Christianity's Compass

THE ORIGIN AND SIGNIFICANCE OF A CONTESTED BIBLE

JAKOB VAN BRUGGEN

Copyright © 2021

ISBN 978-0-9923986-3-7

Pro Ecclesia Publishers
Armadale, Western Australia
www.proecclesia.com.au

First published in the Dutch language as:
Het Kompas van het Christendom. Ontstaan en Betekenis van een Omstreden Bijbel by Dr. Jakob van Bruggen. 2002, Kok, Kampen, the Netherlands.

Translation by Aart Plug, by arrangement with the author.

Unless otherwise indicated, all Scripture quotations and references are taken from *The Holy Bible, English Standard Version.* ESV®
Copyright © 2001 by Crossway Bibles.

Contents

Preface	5
Translator's Preface	6

Chapter 1 Where does the Bible come from?	**8**
The Bible, the reading book of Christians	8
The age of the Old Testament	14
The recognition of the New Testament canon	19
The Bible follows in God's footsteps	42

Chapter 2 The enduring value of the Bible	**54**
Different times	54
A different view of the world	58
Residual value	60
Enduring value for whom?	62
Conclusion	65

Chapter 3 Bible and translation	**66**
Original languages	66
Original text	72
Words	75
Sentences	78
Passages	82
Documents	85
Translation and clarity	93

Chapter 4 Bible and history	**95**
The texts and their time	95
The history of revelation	100
The time of the reader	104
Conclusion	108

Chapter 5   Prophecy and fulfilment – the prophetic word   109
Future prophecy   111
Fulfilment   112
Stages of fulfilment   116
Literal fulfilment?   118
Romans 11:25-32 and the fulfilment of prophecy   121
Prophecy and visions   125

Chapter 6   Discerning the meaning of the text   128
Who makes meaning?   128
The tradition of twofold or fourfold meaning of Scripture   130
The meaningful world behind the text   132
From Bible to songbook   134

Chapter 7   A contested book   138
"Did God really say…?"   139
"They are only human documents!"   142
Reading by one's own light   147
No need for rigid defensiveness   163
Conclusion   177

Endnotes   178

Preface

We live in a time in which the Bible is more easily obtainable than ever before. At the same time, there is growing uncertainty among many Christians about the way the Bible is to be used. The popularization of this book seems to go hand in hand with a serious crisis of confidence. Are the Holy Scriptures really that holy, or are they no more than just human documents? Can an ancient text still be meaningful in our postmodern era?

When readers are in danger of losing their confidence, it is time to start facing up seriously to such questions. Preconceived notions are no great help. Facts are what we need. By exploring current areas of attention around the reading of the Bible, we may discover whether we can still confidently read the Bible in the 21st century.

That is why this book provides an introduction to the origin and the significance of the Bible. It is written with interested readers of the Bible in mind.

In this edition, two earlier publications have been incorporated, revised and amplified: *Het lezen van de bijbel. Een inleiding* (1981) and *Wie maakte de bijbel? Over afsluiting en gezag van het Oude en Nieuwe Testament* (1986). As this material was rewritten, the more technical sections (most notably the appendices) and the study guide that was included in one chapter have been omitted. We have endeavoured to ensure that this revised edition responds better to the interests and educational needs of the 21st century. Teachers or lecturers who intend to use this book as a basic educational text will have to provide their own study assignments and literature to accompany it.

Jakob van Bruggen

Translator's Preface

This translation of Dr van Bruggen's book owes its existence to the initiative of Pro Ecclesia Publishers, an organization within the Free Reformed Churches of Australia. This organization aims to assist in the translation and publication of sound Reformed literature for the benefit of students and other readers in various settings.

Rob Eikelboom, chairman of Pro Ecclesia, took up contact with Dr van Bruggen, and asked for permission to have his *Het Kompas van het Christendom* translated into English.

Having obtained this permission, I was asked to carry out the translation.

At every stage in the process of translation, I had the privilege of frequent and intensive interaction with Dr van Bruggen. I am greatly indebted to him for his continuous stream of corrections, clarifications, suggestions for improvement, and encouraging advice. Thank you also, brother, for your patience and forbearance in seeing this project to its conclusion. I trust that the final product does proper justice to the intent, content and distinctive style of your work.

I acknowledge with thanks the assistance of Dr Dean Anderson, who provided helpful advice in dealing with certain points of subject-specific theological language.

A special thank you also to our daughter Rachel Boersma, who closely read the final draft, ensuring that the language of the translation was as clear and effective as it could be. She may not be a theologian, any more than I am, but her command of felicitous academic English is second to none. Having said that, responsibility for any errors, weaknesses or shortcomings in the translation is mine alone.

Finally, thank you to the team at Pro Ecclesia, whose initiative, financial investment and technical support have made this publication possible.

Wherever possible, existing published translations of works in languages other than English have been used in quotations. These have been referenced and acknowledged in the footnotes. Where existing published translations could not be found, translations of quotations were made by the translator, usually by way of Dutch translations by the author. These are indicated in the footnotes as 'translation mine, AP'.

This translation of Dr van Bruggen's original work appears a full generation after its first publication. It has clearly given the author great pleasure and satisfaction to see that this contribution could find its way to a wider audience. It is our joint prayer that it may continue to be a blessing and benefit to all those who wish to honour the integrity and authority of the inspired and life-giving Word of God. May he give praise to his name in and through this resource.

Aart Plug, translator

CHAPTER 1

Where does the Bible come from?

We live in a time in which the Bible is more easily obtainable than ever before. At the same time, there is growing uncertainty among many Christians about the way the Bible is to be used. The popularization of this book seems to go hand in hand with a serious crisis of confidence. Are the Holy Scriptures really that holy, or are they no more than just human documents? Can an ancient text still be meaningful in our postmodern era?

When readers are in danger of losing their confidence, it is time to start facing up seriously to such questions. Preconceived notions are no great help. Facts are what we need. By exploring current areas of attention around the reading of the Bible, we may discover whether we can still confidently read the Bible in the 21st century.

That is why this book provides an introduction to the origin and the significance of the Bible. It is written with interested readers of the Bible in mind.

The Bible, the reading book of Christians

The Christian faith and the Holy Scriptures

The Bible is the reading book of Christians. It must be added, however, that the Christian faith is not a book-faith. It is the Holy Spirit who turns people into Christians; it is he who works faith in their hearts. Christians will not kiss the book; they kneel before their living Saviour in heaven. It is he that they expect. Christianity is sometimes classified as one of the religions 'of the Book'. That tends to obscure the uniqueness of the Christian faith: true, Christians have a Book, but they believe in a Person. It is really quite striking that the Apostles' Creed is able, in twelve short statements, to describe what Christians believe without once actually mentioning the Bible.

Of course, this does not imply that Christianity is a faith without a book. The world-wide church has its King in heaven, God's Spirit in its heart and the Bible in its hands. Hence, the first thing that others will see is the Bible. It comes as no surprise then, that on a superficial level, Christianity is regarded as a religion 'of the book'.

So many written texts have been brought together into one whole that a special terminology has been devised to summarize this core literature of the church. The most common of these terms is the word *Bible*. The historical origin of this word is fairly self-evident. The texts from which the church read were called '*the* books'; in Greek: *ta Biblia*. That is how the word *Biblia* came to be. We come across it in some earlier editions of the Bible: "*Biblia, that is the entire holy Scripture, containing all the canonical books of the Old and New Testaments.*"

At the same time, this plurality of books is so much regarded as a unity that the collective plural '*Biblia*' gradually was understood to be, and eventually replaced by, the singular 'Bible'. Today, when we think of 'Bible', we have one book in mind. A more technical term for the same thing is *the canon*. This indicates a closed and well-defined collection of prophetic texts that serve as a normative and directive written possession of the Christian church.[1] The church would not be able to confess, with one voice, the twelve articles of the Christian faith if it did not possess the Bible as the common standard for what it believes.

It is striking that the Bible itself does not contain any direct reference to the terms *Bible* or *canon*. It is only later that these terms were assigned to this collection of writings. Still, it would be a mistake to conclude from this absence that the *concept* expressed in the words *Bible* or *canon* cannot be found in the Bible itself. These texts may not have prescribed any specific terminology, but they give us ample cause to adopt this more recent usage. They place us firmly on the path of the "*holy* Scriptures".

In the *first* place, we note that in the Bible those parts of God's revelation that had previously been written down were always referred to in a special manner. The choice of language shows that the authors of the Bible were drawing on what to them was a normative and clearly defined legacy. In spite of the fact that this legacy consisted of a growing variety of texts from different times and authors, they spoke of it as a unified whole. In the book of Deuteronomy, it is impressed upon the people of Israel that they are to keep all the commandments and precepts of the Lord. When Daniel investigates what the prophet Jeremiah has said about the duration of the temple's desolation, he consults *the books* (Daniel 9:2). When on various occasions Baruch records what Jeremiah says, this is regarded as an authoritative whole, on the same level as, for example, Moses' dietary regulations (cf Jeremiah 25:13; 30:2; 36:32; 51:60; Daniel 1:8; 9:10-11).

When Jesus comes into the world, he declares that he has not come to abolish '*the Law or the Prophets*' (Matthew 5:17). And he refers the Jews to '*the Scriptures*' as a well-defined and authoritative entity (John 5:39). Jesus comprehensively identifies the Hebrew canon as *"the Law of Moses and the Prophets and the Psalms"* (Luke 24:44), that is to say: the Hebrew Bible, consisting of the well-known threefold division of law, prophets and writings *(tenach)*. It is to this standard that they may measure the fulfilment that has come in Jesus Christ. The believer Timothy has known *the sacred writings* from childhood (II Timothy 3:15). Peter places the collected writings of Paul on the same level as *the other Scriptures* (II Peter 3:15-16). This terminology, which assigns religious authority to a well-defined whole, provides the foundation for later use of terms such as *Bible* and *canon*.

These terms are expressed in the singular; but even so, the Bible itself uses plural nouns in a singular sense, so that expressions such as '*the holy Scriptures*' (plural) still function to indicate what is also known as 'Scripture' (singular). Peter refers to the whole of the Scriptures when he says, *"every prophecy of Scripture"* (II Peter 1:20).

In the *second* place, we note the firm conviction that stands behind this distinctive language use. It demonstrates the speakers' certainty that behind the variety of prophetic texts there is one Person who acts and speaks. In the past, the fathers were spoken to at many times and in many ways, but on all those occasions it was always God himself who spoke (Hebrews 1:1). Peter says that no prophecy was ever produced by the will of man, but men spoke *from God* as they were carried along by the Holy Spirit (II Peter 1:20). That is why Paul says that all Scripture is breathed out by the Spirit of God (*theopneustos:* II Timothy 3;16). It was truly the Word of God himself that the Old Testament prophets could pass on: *"This is what the LORD says…"*, and in Jesus God himself speaks: *"Truly, truly,* (literally: amen, amen) *I say to you…"*. The apostles know that they write as *"apostles, by the will of God"*. Reverence for the Law and the Prophets, for the Scriptures, does not rest on respect for antiquity or tradition as such, but on reverence for the living God, about whom it was said: *"The lion has roared; who will not fear? The* LORD *God has spoken; who can but prophesy?"* (Amos 3:8).

In the *third* place, the Bible contains God's command to preserve what has been revealed. What God speaks is not just a momentary stimulating intervention in history. It has value for later times, and is useful for those who will live in centuries to come. With his own finger, the Lord engraved the Law onto two stone tablets (Exodus 31:18; Deuteronomy 9:10). Moses and the prophets are instructed to write down some of what is revealed to them. On Patmos, John is obliged to write down his visions, as hard as it might have been for him to find the right words. This command to record in writing what he saw and heard would have been meaningless if it had not been God's intention that later generations should draw on this archive of his revelation. There are times when this command to preserve is stated explicitly, but for those who love God's word, that speaks for itself (John 14:24; Luke 2:19).

The emphasis usually lies not on reverence for the books themselves, but on keeping the commands and preserving the faith that are written in them. And of course, this presupposes that the books in which these commands and promises of God are recorded will themselves be preserved. Jesus commands his apostles that they are to teach all nations *"to observe all that I have commanded you"* (Matthew 28:20). But how would anyone learn to observe Jesus' commands if they could not hear or read them somewhere? Faithfulness to the contents of God's revelation cannot be separated from care for the books of his revelation. We read in the Book of Revelation: *"Blessed is the one who reads aloud the words of this prophecy, and blessed are those who hear, and who keep what is written in it, for the time is near"* (ch 1:3). Peter exhorts us that we *"do well to pay attention to the prophetic word, as to a lamp shining in a dark place, until the day dawns"*

(II Peter 1:19). Once again, these formulations demonstrate: Christians are not 'people of a Book', but they are people *with* a Book. Love for their Lord and the expectation of his coming will make them take good care of the various proclamations of his work.

At stake: The Bible as a book to be read

The fact that the Bible presents itself as a coherent whole has consequences for the way it is to be read. It implies that the various texts in it must be read in conjunction with each other, and the various connections in history and in prophecy must be respected. Paul says that *"whatever was written in former days was written for our instruction"* (Romans 15:4). And Peter says that the prophets took great pains to understand the full meaning of the words that referred to later times, the times of Christ's coming and our redemption (I Peter 1:9-12). The meaning of Scripture is therefore to be found in their coherence, in the whole of revelation. Anyone who wants to interpret the New Testament without taking into account, for example, the prophecies of Isaiah, is working like someone who tries to explain the final chapter of a novel without taking the preceding chapters into account.

The coherence of Scripture will prevent isolated, uncoordinated exegeses of single verses or passages read on their own. In his second letter, Peter says that *"no prophecy was ever produced by the will of man, but men spoke from God as they were carried along by the Holy Spirit"*. And on this statement he bases his contention that *"no prophecy of Scripture comes from someone's own interpretation"* (II Peter 1:20-21). The Greek word Peter uses means *individual*, or *private*. His point is that not a single prophecy may be disconnected from the whole of what the Holy Spirit has entrusted to us. Our apostle Peter here sets out the single most important principle for Bible reading: read the Scripture(s) as a whole, and not just as loose fragments; search for God's meaning, and do not isolate any passages from the other things he has said and done.

For many people today, it is by no means self-evident that the Bible is to be read as a whole. The Bible is regarded more as an anthology than as a unified dossier. In the 19th century, many regarded the Old Testament as no more than the oldest existing collection of religious literature of the Jewish people. And the New Testament was classified as early Christian literature. Bible exegesis was transformed into exploration of the source documents of Jewish and Christian religion and culture. Western European Christianity considers itself to be emancipated, and reads the Bible only as a collection of ancestral documents. But who would still regard a little pile of yellowing documents in the family archives as a coherent written record?

Prevailing 20th century attitudes were rather different from those of the previous century. Current perspectives on the Bible reveal that. It is increasingly approached as a collection of authentic, existential faith experiences from the past. Each Bible author will have his own experience or perspective, but all of these will, in some fashion, relate to the faith. Existential Christianity is searching for resonance in the pages of the Bible. But even so, who would still regard these congealed remnants of earlier faith experiences, heterogeneous and time-bound as they are, as one book?

Around the beginning of the 21st century, a certain reaction arose. The stream of what is known as *canonical criticism* has regained an eye for the coherence of the Bible.[2] To this school of thought, the Bible resembles a tree, with year-by-year growth rings. Each new ring presupposes and is built on the previous one. In this way, each subsequent cycle of prophecy (re)interprets the one that came before, and builds upon it. Within this 'growth model', however, it remains unclear to what extent we may still speak of *holy* Scriptures, passing on what holy men, sent from God, spoke. Does the independent value of the previous Scriptures not get lost by being assimilated in a process of textual growth?

At the background to this variety of perspectives, the question keeps coming back: did God really intend that we should read this collection of Scriptures, what we call 'the Bible', as a unified whole? Or was it perhaps the church of later times that made a selection from a wide variety of texts, bringing them together as one *book*? And isn't this canonization by the church perhaps just the latest development in an ongoing process? If it was the *church* that stands at the origin of the Bible, or if it provided a new *setting* for this earlier collection of Scriptures, are we still bound to it? After all, Councils were not inspired, were they, and might the selections they made not have been humanly one-sided?

These questions also have a bearing on the manner in which we read the Bible. As we read, have we chosen the right context when we read the words of the prophets and apostles in the context of the *book* that we call the Bible?

If it is so that the church is not only the bookbinder, but also the collector, the editor, the one that makes the selection, then must we not conclude that the context of 'the Bible as a book' is not legitimate, or that this at the very least imposes an added value? In that case, we ought to lift the various parts of the Bible out of the whole, *before* we begin to interpret them.

Anyone who reads the Bible in the 21st century cannot avoid this critical attitude towards the canon, which first arose in the 18th century. In this first chapter, we do well to further examine the question relating to the origin of what we call *the Bible*. The answer to this question will determine whether we are still able to read *the Bible*, or if we should limit ourselves to making an inventory of the contents of a variety of divergent and mutually not really coherent texts from various centuries.

The age of the Old Testament

In many handbooks and standard theological texts, we read that the Old Testament, as we find it in the Hebrew Bible and in most Protestant translations, was not really fixed until the end of the first century AD. Moreover, it is often asserted that the book of Daniel itself cannot be dated any earlier than the 2nd century BC, because the prophecies recorded in it are so exact and so concrete that they could not have been written as earlier predictions, but must have been recorded *after* the events that they describe.[3] Further, it is pointed out that the Song of Songs and Ecclesiastes were disputed among Jewish scholars until the first century AD.

This account of events is sometimes – but not always – presented with a specific reference to the fixing of the Old Testament canon at the Council of Jamnia. Around 90 AD a Jewish 'synod' is thought to have taken place at Yavneh (or Jamnia). There a decision is believed to have been made to include the Song of Songs and the book of Ecclesiastes in the canon. Is it true, as this argument would have it, that the Old Testament canon dates from the period after the prophets, and that it was not fixed until after the fall of Jerusalem in 70AD?[4]

Josephus

At the end of the first century AD, the Jewish scholar and historian Flavius Josephus wrote an *apologia* in support of the Jews against a certain Apion. In this work, Josephus also refers to the Jewish sacred texts. From ancient times, he writes, the Jews had taken great pains to preserve the writings of the fathers: it was especially the priests and the prophets who stood guard over them.[5] Aided by divinely inspired insight, the prophets recorded ancient history.[6] That is why the Jews do not have a large number of mutually contradictory texts, as many other peoples do; rather, for them 22 books are sufficient. These books are mutually harmonious and provide an authentic description of ancient Jewish history and laws.[7] Josephus arrives at the number 22 by organizing in a slightly different manner the books that are known to us. Among both Jews and Christians there was one listing of 22 books. (There was another one of 24, but it listed the same books). Josephus states that all of these books were written during the period from Moses to Artaxerxes. They were divided as follows: the Law (the five books of Moses), the Prophets (thirteen books) and the other books (hymns and regulations for daily life).[8] A number of texts from the period of Artaxerxes have also been preserved, but these are considered of lesser value, because they were not part of a continuous and unbroken prophetic succession.[9] Even though many centuries have passed since then, writes Josephus, no-one has dared to add to or subtract from these books.[10] His account completely excludes the possibility of a deliberate fixing of the canon later than the time of Artaxerxes, and also implies that all the books of the Old Testament date from an earlier time. Josephus had a detailed and accurate knowledge of rabbinical discussions of his time: his account does not leave room for the possibility that some of the Old Testament books might still have been disputed as late as the first century AD.

4 Ezra

In an apocalyptic text from the end of the first century AD we find the legend that Ezra, after the Holy Scriptures had been destroyed by fire, wrote down the 24 books with divine help (together with 70 other books, which remained hidden).[11] This legend forms the basis for the contention that Ezra would have been the one who fixed the Old Testament canon. There is, however, nothing in *4 Ezra* that would point in this direction. Ezra only took care of the restoration of what already existed. The legend may explain how the books of the Bible might have been preserved, in spite of the fury of the enemy, and in spite of the fact that the sacred scrolls, kept in the temple, were not preserved when it was destroyed by Nebuchadnezzar.

4 Ezra shows that its author, just as his readers, took the same view about the age of the canon as we encountered with Josephus.

Jesus Sirach

The apocryphal book *Jesus Sirach* records the wisdom of someone who lived in the second century BC. His grandson translated this work into Greek, around the century's end. His prologue to the translation shows that he already knows the threefold division of the Hebrew Old Testament[12], and by implication that he too assumes an established and complete canon of Bible books. He lists them as *"the Law, the prophets and the other books of the fathers"*. He describes how zealously his grandfather would read them: this too implies his assumption that by the beginning of the second century BC these writings were regarded as an established and clearly delineated whole. This grandson of Jesus Sirach was familiar with the Greek translation of the Bible, and he notes that the sacred books speak with greater clarity and force in the Hebrew text than in the – often divergent – translation.

The conclusion is warranted that at the beginning of the second century BC the Old Testament as we know it was already known, used and translated as an established entity.[13]

This conclusion, insofar as it relates to the third group, the 'other books', is challenged by Eissfeldt. In the prologue, Eissfeldt sees no more than 'a beginning' of the formation of the group 'other writings'. Kaiser, too, argues that Jesus Sirach's grandson places his grandfather's work on the same level as these books from the third part of the Bible. The prologue, however, provides no support for these contentions. Just as it refers to *'the* law' and *'the* prophets', we also read of *'the* other books. This threefold use of the definite article leads us to think of three clearly defined groups. The book Jesus Sirach is only comparable to the Bible in relation to the 'loss' that always occurs when a text is translated into another language.

Eissfeldt also states that the book of Daniel can be regarded as an exception[14]. In support of this contention, he refers to the lengthy epilogue in Jesus Sirach, in which the entire history of Israel is recounted by means of a succession of blessings upon its great men. In this recital, Isaiah, Jeremiah and Ezekiel are listed, as are the twelve minor prophets (as a group, and as such already included in the canon!), but Daniel is not.

Over against this, it is worth noting that the prophets are not listed in their usual order. When Hezekiah is praised (48:17-25), Isaiah receives a mention, because it is through him that prayer is heard (48:20). After the praise of Josiah, the last righteous king (49:1-3) the decline and destruction of Israel is described in summary. Jeremiah is mentioned in the context of the destruction of Jerusalem, which followed as a punishment upon his arrest (49:7). Ezekiel is mentioned because he, in this time, reminds Israel of the holiness of God and the righteousness of Job (49:8,9). The twelve minor prophets, too, are named, *"for they comforted the people of Jacob and delivered them with confident hope"* (49:10, NRSV). In this context, which gives an account of the godly and ungodly walk of the people, there is no reason to mention Daniel. Daniel is not a prophet among Israel, speaking to the people and calling them to repentance. Jesus Sirach doesn't follow the list of Bible books; rather, he weaves together names that fit into his story and its purpose. The fact that he does not mention Daniel does not imply that this prophet was unknown to him.

The Samaritan Bible

It is often pointed out that the Samaritans only acknowledge the five books of Moses. After the Babylonian exile, there was a parting of ways of the Samaritans with Israel: they built their sanctuary on Mount Gerizim. Would the date of this schism point to a late growth of the Old Testament? Should we not deduce from this event that the formation of the canon had at that point not progressed beyond the five books of Moses? This could mean, then, that the prophets and the other books would have not been brought together and established until the centuries after this parting of ways at the earliest (in other words, around the third century BC).

However, against this line of thinking the following objection could be raised. The breach with the Samaritans had very deep roots. The pivotal moment was the division of the 12 tribes after the death of Solomon. From that time on, the kingdom of the ten tribes went its own way, broke with the temple in Jerusalem, set up its own place of worship, and had its own prophets (I Kings 12-13). After the ten tribes were carried off into exile, pagan peoples were brought in, and a priest from the northern kingdom was brought in to teach them some rudiments concerning the worship of the local God. It seems reasonable to think that this instruction led, at best, to the kind of worship that prevailed in the pre-Solomonic period, and further to a negation of Jerusalem and a disregard for the prophets from Judah (I Kings 17:24-41). After the exile, the returning Jews had refused, from the beginning, to collaborate with these Samaritans: it is clearly incorrect, then, to create the impression that the schism between Israel and the Samaritans did not occur till some time after the return from exile. The schism that already existed was simply reinforced. The fact that Samaritans would only accept the five books of Moses – and that in an ancient script that dated from before the exile! – came about because of the division of the kingdom after Solomon. The kingdom of the ten tribes had always been hostile to David and Solomon (and their Scriptures), and its people had simply not accepted the prophetic voices and historiography that came from Jerusalem.

In relation to the dating of the Old Testament, there is one positive aspect to the Samaritan Bible: clearly, the five books of Moses had already been accepted by all tribes, long before the reign of David and Solomon, as the Word of God.

Conclusion

Whatever is known from history about the functioning of the Hebrew canon of the Old Testament as we know it gives us ample reason to conclude that it was already established before the period of Jesus Sirach (the second century BC). It is impossible to point to any assembly or event at which this canon would have been determined at some later date by means of a human decision.

This is an important conclusion. For example, it refutes the generally accepted view that the book of Daniel was written some time in the second century BC, as a 'prophecy-after-the-fact', and not in the sixth century BC as a 'prophecy-before-the-fact'. It also refutes the thought that the Holy Scriptures would only gradually have taken on a separate identity from national Jewish literature in the centuries after the exile, and in part would have been written, compiled or established during that later period.

It is evident, then, that the Old Testament is as old as its most recent book dates itself.

The recognition of the New Testament canon

During the 19th century a trend developed of dating an increasing number of New Testament books *later* than had always been believed. Letters and gospels were shifted to the second century. It was argued that the process of recording the tradition about Jesus would not have begun till quite late, and that quite a few New Testament letters were inauthentic products, dating from the second and third centuries AD. During the 20th century these supposedly late datings were largely challenged, and a growing consensus emerged that (almost) all of the gospels and letters were written during the first century.

However, this partial or complete return to earlier datings did not mean that the recognition of the New Testament as a canonical unity was also brought back to the first century. The dominant view is still that there is a large time interval between the *production* of the letters on the one hand, and their *recognition* as a collected and established whole on the other. Initially, so goes the argument, the literary production of Christians would not have been regarded as having the same value as the Bible (the Old Testament). It was only when a number of Christian texts began to be regarded as authoritative, that a trend gradually emerged to create, next to the established canon (the Old Testament), another (distinctively Christian) canon or Bible. In this way, by means of a lengthy process of development, the New Testament eventually took shape: a second Bible, next to the first. And while the books that are included in the New Testament may be relatively old, perhaps as old as the first century AD, the exclusive and authoritative selection that we have today would not have begun to develop any earlier than the second century, or have been finally established until the fourth century.

According to this dominant view, it could therefore be said that the New Testament is actually a relatively recent collection of older books. Even Trobisch himself, who on the basis of the manuscripts concludes that the New Testament was already edited as a single book at an early date, has to acknowledge that for the time being he is still a lonely exception to the prevailing view.[15]

While there may be all kinds of variations in the reconstruction of the history of the origin of the New Testament, it is possible to draw a sketch of often-recurring broad outlines. There is a level of agreement among the Bible scholars who subscribe to this view in relation to the following key moments in the history of the New Testament. It goes something like this:

1. Paul's letters were probably already collected into anthologies, and it is likely that (a variety of) written gospels (some in their current form, others not) were already in circulation, but the church was still living by the authority of the Scriptures (the Old Testament) without the presence of an additional or supplementary *written* authority. Next to the long-established Bible stood the authority of the risen Lord, about whom a number of traditions had been passed on. Even if those traditions had been partly or wholly fixed in writing, these established writings (the gospels and the letters) did not assume the authority upon which the faith was based or appealed to. In this time of a still living oral tradition, there was not yet any need for the formation of a Christian Bible next to the Old Testament.

2. This need is supposed to have been awakened when, in the middle of the second century, the heretic Marcion began to assemble a wholly self-selected 'Christian Bible' (the gospel of Luke, and ten of Paul's letters). This challenged the church to engage in reflection concerning the value and the extent of its spiritual inheritance. There had to be a better way of making an inventory of its texts and organizing them. This is where the establishment of the canon is said to have begun (or at least more consciously pursued), and here, drawing on a multitude of documents, the New Testament is said to have gradually taken shape. It is at the end of the second century that we begin to encounter specific references by Christian writers to the books of the New Testament. And next to the Old Testament, a New Testament also begins to function as 'Holy Scripture'.

3. The definitive completion of this new Christian Bible is supposed to have taken place in the fourth century AD. Influential leaders such as Athanasius and the synods of the prominent church province of North Africa (393 and 397AD) are said to have answered and silenced any lingering questions and doubts about the true delineation of the New Testament.

Now it is not so that these three pivotal points in the history of the establishment of the New Testament can readily and without debate be deduced from historical sources. Rather, we are dealing here with a (fairly generally accepted) reconstruction, making use of fragmentary data from the writings of church authors on the one hand, and the interpretations and hypotheses of scholars on the other.

Does this hypothetical reconstruction do justice to the facts? To begin with, there is no complete and ready-to-hand historical account of events during the first centuries of the church that could conclusively refute this reconstruction. Our sources are too fragmentary and too incomplete for that. But even though there will always be blank spaces on the map, which no-one is ever likely to completely fill in, the question may be asked whether the course of events as briefly portrayed above is a plausible one. Does it not clash with what we *do* know, and does it provide a valid interpretation of the data that we *do* have?

The answer to such questions is significant. After all, if it is true that the canon is a tailored product of the church in the second to fourth centuries, the question arises why we should consider ourselves more bound to this New Testament than to other literature from the ancient Christian era. A wholly different light falls on the books contained in the New Testament if its collection and organization was not inherent to the books themselves, but externally imposed by a strange hand. When the New Testament lets go of the label 'Bible', we will certainly deal differently with the books that are in it.

In the sections to follow, we will critically examine each of the three pivotal points, in order to answer the question whether the currently prevailing view can be sustained as tenable, or not. But even if we should arrive at a critical re-evaluation of the prevailing model, this does not yet mean that we should be compelled to propose another, complete reconstruction to take its place.

The church has for many centuries already accepted the New Testament as authoritative. Not that its authority needs to be proved, but the doubts cast by the critical-historic approach on its authority ought to be tested. In past centuries the church has never accepted the authority of the New Testament *on the basis of* a historical reconstruction of its origins.

The church's recognition has always rested on a different foundation (see section 4 of this chapter). It would therefore not be proper if this recognition were to be undermined on the basis of a historical reconstruction of the history of the canon, compelling us to strive for a *historical* justification of our faith in the authority of the Bible. It is more appropriate to limit ourselves to testing the proposed historical reconstruction itself. Just because a city might be unable to provide a precise date when it was awarded its civic charter, that does not yet mean that doubts can be cast on the existence of these rights themselves. Were someone to attempt to dispute these rights on the basis of a particular reconstruction of its history, the refutation of this reconstruction need not require the presentation of an exact date!

The post-apostolic generation

Historical perspective

Not many documents written by Christians around the end of the first century AD and the beginning of the second have been preserved for us. The Christian authors of this period are often referred to as the "Apostolic Fathers" (Clement, Ignatius, Barnabas, Hermas, and others). Were we to gather all the texts of the apostolic fathers and all other Christian literature from this period (the *Didache*, fragments of Papias' writings) into one anthology, we would be left with a relatively small volume. It is a scant harvest compared to the massive folios in which the texts of ecclesiastic authors from around 200 AD are preserved. When we compare the extensive body of works of Tertullian, Irenaeus, Clement of Alexandria and Origen (all produced just before or just after 200 AD) with the small volume in which all the writings of the Apostolic Fathers are gathered (around 100 years earlier), then it is not surprising that there are more references to the New Testament dating from around 200 AD than from 100 AD!

There is more. Not only is there a great *quantitative* difference between the Apostolic Fathers and later authors; there is also an important *qualitative* difference. At the beginning of the second century, the martyr Ignatius, on his way to the arena in Rome, wrote moving letters to churches, with the aim of exhorting them to remain unified and steadfast around their leaders. At the end of the first century, Clement, the leader of the church in Rome, wrote a letter to the sister church in Corinth, addressing divisions that threatened between the elders and the younger generation. The letter of Barnabas, dating from the same period, is devoted to a Christian exegesis of the Old Testament. And Hermas' *Shepherd* (from the end of the first century) contains numerous visions and prophecies, exhorting believers in the church to live holy lives. All of these texts are *internal* to the church and aimed at safeguarding the Christian community. And that is why it is not surprising that there is little to be found in them about the origins of the New Testament. The matters at stake at that time were the holiness of life and the maintenance of Christian unity: it is quite reasonable that these letters would not contain any explicit statements concerning the authority or the extent of the canon. The writings of the Old Covenant, Jesus' commandments and the words of the apostles function within these earliest documents. Still, there is little that can be deduced from them about the extent of the Old Testament, or the manner in which Jesus' words and the teachings of the apostles had been preserved. These were matters of common knowledge. The church knew well enough how authoritative material, both written and oral, was to be regarded: all we see is how they were put to use in correspondence among the churches.

A century later, things were quite different. Theologians such as Clement of Alexandria, Origen and Tertullian wrote – just as Irenaeus did – much more with unbelievers and heretics in mind. One would expect that in such a setting there would be much more explicit and deliberate consideration of all kinds of matters – including the canon. It is in these works, then, that we find much more information about the Bible books they referred to.

This brings with it the risk of a distortion of perspective: it might appear that in the generation immediately following the apostles less was written about the canon because there was less of it. However, that need not be the case. When explicit information about the canon begins to emerge more clearly around 200 AD, this is easily explained by the quantitative and qualitative differences between our sources dating back to 100 AD and 200 AD respectively. We ought to take care that we do not ask too much of the next generation after the apostles: they had other concerns to think about than theoretical considerations about the way the Bible was used and how it came to be. Just because the Apostolic Fathers did not write about something does not yet mean that there was nothing available at the time!

No Scriptural authority outside of the Old Testament Scriptures?

Where the Old Testament was usually referred to in the writings of the Apostolic Fathers as the *written* word ('it is written', 'Scripture says') we do not – as a rule – see Jesus' own statements and the words of the apostles referred to in the same way. They are often quoted, but usually in a manner that leaves it unclear whether these statements are taken from a written source, or loosely quoted from the author's memory and on the authority of an oral tradition.

While it may be true that 20th century scholars have been less likely than their 19th century counterparts to state that written gospels did not yet exist, they have often asserted that Jesus' words and the apostles' commands were recognized, not because they were contained in some kind of Bible, but because they had been passed on directly from the Lord who had spoken with authority in his church.

This is a subtle and yet important difference. Von Campenhausen puts it this way: *"The authority that stands behind* (quotations from Jesus and the apostles) *is still – just as with Paul – the authority of the Lord himself, and not the authority of a special written document, regarded as 'canonical', in which his words were preserved and could be found."*[16] Von Campenhausen means that while Jesus' words did have authority, and were regarded on the same level as what was written in the Old Testament, the Old Testament quotations had authority because they were *Scripture*. That was not yet so for Jesus' words: they were highly regarded, not because they were recorded in a Bible, but because they were *Jesus'* words.

The dilemma that emerges here requires careful analysis. On the one hand, it can be noted that also today the church accepts Jesus' words in the Bible because they are *Jesus'* words, and not because they are found in the Bible. After all, the Bible also contains words of godless people, and false prophets: the church does not accept them as having authority over doctrine or life. It is *Jesus' authority*, and that of the apostles, that sanctifies the words of the Bible. It is not so that the Bible sanctifies everything that is written in it. To that extent, there is nothing unusual about the Apostolic Fathers, in their time, submitting to the direct authority of Jesus himself: after all, they confess him as the Christ, the Son of the living God. That is why his words are regarded as having authority! If things are as they should be, nothing has changed within Christianity at this point.

But now, the dilemma that Von Campenhausen presents suggests that the reverence for Jesus' authority did not yet assign the *authority of Scripture* to the New Testament gospels and letters that the Old Testament had already received. Outside of (Old Testament) Scripture there may be authority, but it is not yet the 'authority of Scripture'.

It could be asked whether first century Christians already grasped this abstraction. Would anyone who read a word of Jesus in one of the gospels, and who trembled before it because it was clothed with the authority of the living Lord, not also tremble before 'what was written'? Is there any real difference between the manner in which the reader showed respect for a prophecy from the Old Testament Scriptures and the manner in which he received a word from Jesus in one of the gospels? Anyone who reflects on Von Campenhausen's subtle dilemma will not be able to escape the impression that this is a dilemma from a later period, which has been imposed here upon an era in which it does not fit. This impression is likely to be confirmed when we consider the facts more closely.

Scripture quotations

The thought that the first post-apostolic generation assigned *Scriptural* authority only to the Old Testament, and that the letters and gospels that circulated in this period lacked such an authorization, seems to find strong support in the manner in which quotations were introduced. Quotes from the Old Testament are usually presented as 'words of Scripture', while the words Jesus spoke are generally introduced with expressions that point to what Jesus *said* ("he says", "Jesus says" etc). The interpretation given to this phenomenon does not, however, do justice to all of the facts.

a. It was customary to refer to the Old Testament as 'the Scriptures', and it was generally referred to with the introduction "*as it is written*". After only one generation, such a reference may not yet have been in general use for *all* of the authoritative Scriptures of the new Testament church. But that is a matter of current usage, which often persists for some time. However, this usage need not lead to the conclusion that a different *value* was assigned to the Old Testament (the Scriptures) than to the gospels and letters (which at that time were not yet referred to or quoted in terms that were normal for the Old Testament).

b. Besides, there is no absolute contrast between two different forms of quotation. Quite often, words from the Old Testament are referred to with formulae such as 'the prophet *says*' (see, for example Barnabas IV:4, VI:6,7, IX:8, XI 2:4). No-one would contend, on the basis of these differences, that in such cases the prophet's authority counts for more than the written word.

There is, after all, a much more likely explanation. In the great majority of cases, people only knew the Bible as it was read to them. The words of Scripture were to them always the words that they *heard*. Much more than today, Scripture entered the minds of people through their *ears* rather than their *eyes*. The expressions used by the authors to introduce quotations to their audiences (letters and visions that were read aloud!) bear traces of that. In addition, when Jesus' words were read aloud from a gospel to the *congregation*, to this audience they were *spoken* words. By the mouth of the officiating reader, the Lord spoke to them. The written and the spoken word overlapped.

The fact that Jesus' words also came to them in *written* texts is evident in that the formula that was commonly used for the Old Testament also occurs occasionally in a quotation of Jesus' words. Barnabas IV:14 has: "*As it is written: many are called, but few are chosen*"[17]. And in II Clement II:4 it reads: "*And another word from Scripture* (graphè) s*ays: I have not come to call the righteous, but sinners*"[18]. And as early as in the *Didache* (VIII:2) we find a formula that is hard to understand unless we think of a Gospel that is read aloud: "*But as the Lord commanded in his gospel: pray thus…*" (then follows the Lord's Prayer in connection with – just as in Matthew 6 – words about fasting).

From the formulas used in quotations such as these, it is clear that in the time of the Apostolic Fathers there was no differentiation between the Old Testament (the Scriptures from of old) and the gospels and the letters. Substantially they were considered equivalent, and the terminology used was sometimes the same.

Books and letters already held in honour?

In the generation immediately following the apostolic period, writers apparently already worked from fixed texts of the gospels. This seems clear from their allusions to facts as recorded in the gospels that are known to us. Without any further elaboration, Ignatius[19] refers to the oil that was poured over Jesus' head (Ephesians XVII:1, cf. Matthew 26:7). He assumes that everyone would have known that the birth of Jesus was kept hidden from the ruler of this world (Ephesians XIX:1, cf Matthew 2:8,12). He also elaborates on the appearance of the star to the Magi on the way to Bethlehem (Ephesians XIX:2-3, cf. Matthew 2:2,9-10). In his letter to Philadelphia, Ignatius refers to words from John 3:8. These and other allusions could only have functioned within a community in which the tradition about Jesus' life had already been fixed in one of more written accounts that were commonly known.

In this context, II Clement XIV:2 is very clear. First the author quotes from "Scripture" (the Old Testament), after which he also appeals to "the books of the apostles". Here he draws on something *next to* the Old Testament, namely the books of the gospels (plural!) and (the writings of) the apostles.

> *"And I do not suppose ye are ignorant that the living Church is the body of Christ: for the scripture saith, 'God made man, male and female'. The male is Christ and the female is the Church. And the Books and the Apostles plainly declare that the Church existeth not now for the first time, but hath been from the beginning: for she was spiritual, as our Jesus also was spiritual, but was manifested in the last days that He might save us."*

In the course of the argument, a first reference to Jesus' manifestation in the flesh continues with a quotation from Paul's first letter to the Corinthians. It is clear then, that the author substantiates his argument from the books (the gospels) and the apostles (the letters). This passage clearly demonstrates that a false dilemma is introduced when one suggests that living by the authority of the living Lord did not (yet) coincide with the use, on the same level as the Old Testament, of the gospels and the letters.

No second Bible

When we look back from a period in which we have the Old and New Testaments bound together in one volume, as two parts of one Bible, it is easy for us to forget that both of these parts undoubtedly have authority, but that their historical contours are different. This was much more obvious to the apostles and to the generation that immediately followed them than it is to us. The early Christians did not believe that the Bible (the Old Testament) needed to be supplemented by a second part (the New

Testament); rather, they believed that the truth of the Bible (the Old Testament) came to expression and found its realization in the coming of Jesus and the work of the apostles. The new was in fact not new at all, but very old. The Bible was not expanded, but *fulfilled*.

The fact that the texts in which this fulfilment is described function with the same authority does not yet mean that in the time of the Apostolic fathers they were positioned on exactly the same level as the Old Testament, in a manner that would cause their readers to forget their relative difference in historical contours. Because at that time the discussion with non-Christian Jews was still ongoing, people were still reminded of the remarkable situation that the common Bible (the Old Testament) was, for one group, cause to reject the Gospel, while for the other it was precisely the justification for believing in the Gospel.

In Ignatius' letter to the Philadelphians (VIII, 2) this comes to expression very clearly. Ignatius appeals to his readers not to quarrel, but to hold fast to the doctrine of Christ. For Ignatius himself, following Christ is to be taken completely for granted. He substantiates his argument by briefly reminding them of a discussion with a number of quarrelsome Jews.

> *"For I heard certain persons saying, If I find it not in the charters* (ancient writings, tr.)*, I believe it not in the Gospel. And when I said to them, 'It is written', they answered me, 'That is the question'. But as for me, my charter is Jesus Christ, the inviolable charter is His cross and His death and His resurrection, and faith through Him; wherein I desire to be justified through your prayers".*[20]

Ignatius' opponents disputed the authority of the gospel. They wanted to find it all in the 'ancient charters'. By this they meant the Old Testament. These are characterized as the 'ancient charters' in contrast to the recent books, in particular the gospels. The Gospel, too, has been written down: one might just as well 'find' something in it as in the ancient writings. That is why you cannot, in this context, simply call the Old Testament 'the Scriptures'. Ignatius' opponents have chosen a name for the Old Testament that emphasizes their age, and so distinguishes them from books containing 'new teachings'. Ignatius now points out to them that the whole truth of the Gospel was already written down in their Old Testament. In their resistance to the Gospel, they in fact close their eyes to the true meaning of the ancient texts. But that is not what Ignatius does. As far as he is concerned, the Old Testament is none other than Christ, and faith in him. As he continues with this passage, Ignatius increasingly emphasizes that the Old Testament already pointed to the High Priest as the door to God. Now, the Gospel gives an account of the coming, the suffering and the resurrection of Christ. But the beloved ancient prophets of the Old Testament had already proclaimed their gospel with an eye to him.

Ignatius' train of thought gives us the opportunity to place ourselves within the spiritual climate of the first century AD. Why does it often seem as if there is no New Testament next to the Old? Because at all times the books and letters of recent times were regarded as an explication of the books of the Old Covenant. Sometimes, that may create the impression as if the New Testament writings were not held in honour, but if that is what we think we lose sight of the special *manner* in which the New Testament Scriptures were held in honour. Not as a *second* Bible next to the old one, but as authoritative writings in which the ancient Scriptures have now clearly and definitively come to full expression.

Where a uniform publication of the Old and New Testaments in one volume may to a degree mask this difference in historical contours, that is regrettable. However, a restoration of this difference does not impinge on the authority of either the Old or the New.

Written tradition

As regards the gospels and the epistles, there is one other aspect in which the perspective of the post-apostolic generation was different. For us, who live many centuries later, the tide of the New Testament texts has, in a manner of speaking, gone out. The first readers of these texts were still surrounded by the backwash of what was passed on orally. In a certain sense, the gospels are nothing else than the written tradition about Jesus, and the epistles are actually the written tradition of the apostles. They do not contain the whole tradition, or the sum total of all that the apostles passed on. In a period in which unwritten traditions were still circulating, the texts can be more easily regarded as fixed versions of this oral tradition: just as trustworthy, but more limited in extent. The written text cannot tell us more than what was actually recorded on paper. In a period in which there is more to be heard, such limitations would be more noticeable than in a later period, when the reliable spokespeople of the oral tradition are no longer present.

We encounter this phenomenon very clearly with Papias (from the beginning of the 2nd century AD). He wrote five books, in which he presents a commentary on the stories about Jesus. Regrettably, almost all of this work has been lost, and there are only a few fragments left. The most important of these fragments have been preserved in Eusebius' *History of the Church*. We can be sure that Papias' commentary focused chiefly on the gospels. This we can conclude from the fact that Eusebius drew on Papias' record of Matthew and Mark. In his commentary, Papias drew on their gospels, and he goes to considerable trouble to explain their distinctive characteristics by providing information about the authors and their intentions.[21] It is clearly incorrect to conclude that Papias only discussed a loose collection of orally circulating words of Jesus, or that he drew on a – to us – unknown source which only contained the words of Jesus. Papias also had written texts to draw on.

Now it is striking how Papias set to work in preparing his commentary. While modern exegetes must confine themselves to the text itself, Papias gathered information from those who had personally known Jesus, or who had themselves heard the apostles speak. Papias considered this oral tradition – insofar as it was still available to him – to be a valuable help for his work. He writes:

> "But I shall not hesitate also to put down for you along with my interpretations whatsoever things I have at any time learned carefully from the elders (the first generation after the apostles, VB) and carefully remembered, guaranteeing their truth. For I did not, like the multitude, take pleasure in those that speak much, but in those that teach the truth; not in those that relate strange commandments, but in those that deliver the commandments given by the Lord to faith, and springing from the truth itself. If then, any one came, who had been a follower of the elders, I questioned him in regard to the words of the elders— what Andrew or what Peter said, or what was said by Philip, or by Thomas, or by James, or by John, or by Matthew, or by any other of the disciples of the Lord, and what things Aristion and the presbyter John, the disciples of the Lord, say. For I did not think that what was to be gotten from the books would profit me as much as what came from the living and abiding voice."[22]

This last sentence has given some scholars reason to conclude that Papias considered the gospels to be of lesser value than the oral tradition. Such a conclusion, however, is at odds with the very fact that Papias is writing a commentary on the gospels: clearly, he deems them significant enough to interpret them. To him the question was: did he, in his time, have to be satisfied with what he finds in the gospels, or did he believe that in order to fully understand the gospels, reliable information that comes directly from the Lord himself would be very useful? Clearly, the latter is true. Papias the exegete is only too aware that hunching over the books themselves will give him less insight than putting his ear to the ground at the Source himself. After all, for him, what counts is what the Lord *himself* had said: his is the *'living and abiding voice'* through which we are born again (here, Papias is clearly alluding to I Peter 1:23). Papias highly esteems the books (the gospels), because they contain the words and acts of Jesus, but for him he values even more what he (by way of the oral tradition) can learn directly from the Lord himself. No-one who goes to draw water from the well itself would deny that the water gathered in jars is still real water, and can really quench one's thirst! It would be wrong to interpret Papias' exegetical interest in the ancient oral tradition about Jesus as a canonical devaluation of the written gospels. Why else would he go to the trouble of explaining them to his congregation?

Summary

The limited extent and the internally-directed character of Christian literature in the period immediately following the departure of the apostles hinders us from gaining a clear picture of the extent and spread of the New Testament in this early period.

It is clear, however, that intensive use was made of information and of the tradition that was passed on by means of the present New Testament. In addition, the formulas commonly used when quoting from the Old Testament were sometimes also used to introduce quotations from one of the Gospels. It appears to be certain that, next to the Old Testament, the '*books* (the gospels) *and* (the writings of) *the apostles'* were regarded as an authoritative source.

The difference between the manner in which the New Testament writings are quoted from the way the Old Testament is used is not connected to the (supposedly) lesser authority of the gospels and the letters. Rather, it has two other causes: first, it arises from the differences in historical contours between the Old Testament and their fulfilment in Jesus and the apostles; second, it reflects the circumstance that the gospels and the letters were still embedded in an oral tradition that went back directly to Jesus and the apostles themselves.

Looking back, as we do from the 21st century, with its clearly defined canon of the Bible, the distant picture (the post-apostolic generation) has become hazy. This absence of clarity does not, however, imply that the historical line of the canon only began in the second century AD. The information we have about the Apostolic Fathers gives us no grounds to think so. Historical developments during the latter part of the 2nd century will provide us with the means to test this conclusion. If evidence can be produced that the church made an intentional transition during the 2nd century from faith in the living Lord to one based on written documents, that might give us reason to reconsider what the situation might have been around 100AD. If, however, no trace can be found of such a sudden transition, then that would serve as an after-the-fact confirmation that the history of the canon already began in the first century, even if it might be difficult to gain a clear picture of this historical beginning.

Marcion's Bible (The middle of the 2nd Century AD)

Marcion, a wealthy shipowner from Sinope (in Pontus, on the Black Sea coast in present-day Turkey) was the founder of the first counter-church, which was established next to and in opposition to the Catholic Christian church. This movement had its own doctrine, its own organization, its own liturgy, and above all: its own canon. This sect began to develop independently around 150AD, soon after Marcion's teachings had been repudiated by the church in Rome. Marcionite churches were widespread: the polemic against Marcion makes reference to a spread of this community throughout the Roman world. The influence of this counter-church was at its greatest during the second half of the 2nd century. It is not for nothing that leaders such as Tertullian and Irenaeus went to great lengths to oppose this new teaching.

At the heart of Marcion's theology was a strong separation between the Creator (the demiurge, Yahweh of the old covenant: a god of action, judgement and retribution) and the Redeemer (the God of goodness and love, revealed in Jesus). Marcion rejected the Old Testament: in any case it could not be regarded as the revelation of the good God. On the other hand, he was a strong adherent of Paul (at least as he understood this apostle). This led to a 'canon of Paul', which consisted of two parts: 1. The gospel of Luke (Paul's companion); 2. Ten letters of Paul (excluding those to Timothy and Titus). Those parts of the text that contradicted Marcion's teaching (a fair amount), he changed or deleted. For example, the first chapters of Luke are missing, while Paul's letters contain numerous 'corrections' and smaller omissions.

In the past 150 years, Marcion's activity has often been regarded as one of the chief catalysts of the maturing process of the early church. Von Harnack, who produced a renowned and much-discussed study of Marcion,[23] proposed that the whole idea of a canon originated with Marcion, and that it was later taken over and worked out more broadly by the early church. John Knox, a leading 20th century theologian, was also a well-known proponent of this theory.[24] Since then, many have toned down this position, but most scholars still accept that Marcion cannot be left out of the history of the canon. At the very least, he is thought to have stimulated, if not originated, the development of a closed canon.[25]
Th. Zahn, a knowledgeable opponent of Von Harnack in the study of the canon, has attempted to show in great detail that Marcion did nothing more than strengthen the church's awareness of its long-held heritage. Zahn's work, however, received little recognition, and therefore even E.C. Blackman, a more moderate scholar, regards Marcion as the first one to create a 'closed canon', which contained a '*fixed* number' of books.[26] True, Blackman takes the view that the New Testament came into being more by 'selection' than by 'collection', but still, a selection of this kind would probably not have occurred (or have occurred later), were it not for Marcion.

Is it after all true, then, that we have the holy men of God to thank for the Scriptures, and the bound one-volume Bible to the challenge Marcion posed? While this impression has been created from various directions, it must raise serious objection, the core of which is that Marcion's opponents accused him of mutilating the Scriptures. He is the one who "*interpolated (altered) the evangelical and apostolic Scriptures*" (Origen).[27] How could Marcion be denounced as the one who mutilated Scripture, if there was not yet something to mutilate? Marcion was not attacked as a believer who made one-sided selections, but as a man who laid sacrilegious hands on the possession of the church. Not merely textual interferences within one text, but the omission of entire books and letters. Omissions, moreover, that could be characterised not as negligence, but as a deliberate violation of what already existed. For Marcion's criticism to make sense, the idea of a canon must already have been firmly established before he came onto the scene. Perhaps there might have been minor regional differences and marginal variations (such as with the smaller catholic epistles), but this does not detract from the existence of a *closed* New Testament revelation with a demonstrably fixed number of books and letters going back to a time before Marcion's interference began.

Tertullian, who in his *Adversus Marcionem* wrote a very extensive refutation of Marcion's teaching[28] (this has been preserved for us in an expanded edition Tertullian produced to replace various earlier and shorter publications), characterized Marcion as a mouse, gnawing at the canon:

> *"What Pontic mouse ever had such gnawing powers as he who has gnawed the Gospels to pieces?".*

Not only did Marcion recast all the gospels into one text; he also reduced the number of Paul's letters:

> *"... the garbled form in which we have found the heretic's Gospel will have already prepared us to expect to find the epistles also mutilated by him with like perverseness – and that even as respects their number"* (V 1,9).

> *"I wonder, however, when he received into his Apostolicon this letter (Philemon) which was written but to one man, that he rejected the two epistles to Timothy and the one to Titus, which all treat of ecclesiastical discipline. His aim, was, I suppose, to carry out his interpolating process even to the number of (St. Paul's) epistles"* (V 21,1).

It is understandable that this matter receives special attention in the discussion about the gospels and Paul's letters: after all this was the focal point of the confrontation with Marcion. It would be incorrect, however, to assume that before the emergence of this heretic the canon had not yet crystallized beyond these two points (the gospels and Paul). Incidentally, evidence shows that there was more in Tertullian's Bible than these books. At the beginning of the fifth book of his treatise, Tertullian challenges Marcion to show which credentials he has for adopting Paul. How does he legitimize his choice? Tertullian does have such evidence to present: all kinds of Old Testament types and figures already point to Paul. Of course, that would be no help in Tertullian's rebuttal of Marcion, because Marcion had already thrown the Old Testament overboard.

> *"Should you, however, disapprove of these types, the Acts of the Apostles, at all events, have handed down to me this career of Paul, which you must not refuse to accept" (V 1,6).*

Tertullian drives a separation between Marcion and Paul, because Marcion is unable to authenticate the apostle, while the church *can* supply such an authentication, with an appeal to the Book of Acts, for it recounts the story of Paul's conversion. Evidently, the Book of Acts was regarded by the early church on the same level as anything that could be brought to bear from the Old Testament: it had equal authority.

A second example of the recognition of more books in the period before Marcion can be found in IV 5,2: Here, Tertullian mentions in passing that the heretic treats the Revelation of John with contempt.

Already before the middle of the 2nd century, the church possessed not only four gospels and thirteen letters of Paul, but also other books, such as Acts and Revelation.

It is an important question, however, whether these texts were regarded merely as valuable sources of information, or (perhaps without using the word) as a whole, as the canon. It is clear that the latter is true, for we note that Tertullian calls not only the Old Testament an *instrumentum*, but speaks in the same manner about the New Testament also. This overarching terminology demonstrates an awareness of the canon. At the beginning of his fourth book, Tertullian sets out to attack Marcion with his own sword (the gospel of Luke). In doing so, he will deal further with Marcion's book *Antitheseis:* in this work, contrasts are set between the creator-god of the Old Testament, and the God of the new covenant. Each *instrumentum* or *testamentum* is assigned its own deity. Tertullian does acknowledge that there are different dispensations, but he insists that both of them are under the rule of the same God. In this connection Tertullian also speaks about the books that belong to each dispensation:

CHAPTER 1

> *"I do not deny that there is a difference in the language of their documents, in their precepts of virtue, and in their teachings of the law; but yet all this diversity is consistent with one and the same God, even Him by whom it was arranged and also foretold" (IV 1,3).*

How could anyone equate Christian literary texts with a fixed and delineated Old Testament, if the church of the new dispensation did not already possess and recognize a delineated canon? In fact, the opposite is true: from the beginning, the whole concept of a canon is firmly rooted in the conviction that God had provided two dispensations, each with its own *instrumentum*. These two may then be compared as follows:

> *"…the New Testament is compendiously short, and freed from the minute and perplexing burdens of the law" (IV 1,6).*

How would Tertullian have made a statement that alludes to the extent of the New Testament, unless he took his starting point in a closed unity of New Testament revelation? It is clear that Tertullian really does have the whole New Testament in mind, and not just the gospels, for a little later, in 2,1, he explicitly limits himself to the *evangelicum instrumentum*.

A great deal is to be learned from the way Tertullian views the whole of the New Testament writings. Since he usually refers to short, loose and selected quotes, it makes sense to take in the atmosphere of a longer text also. We complete this section with a brief summary of Tertullian's chain of thought in the passage below (IV 2-5):

IV 2: The authors of the gospels are the apostles themselves (Matthew and John), or their close companions (Mark and Luke). Marcion, who omits the beginning of Luke, has no authentication for his gospel. If he were to want to legitimize himself through Paul, he would still need to present a supporting authority to authenticate Paul (compare Galatians 1).

IV 3: Marcion assumes that the other apostles have erred (Galatians 2:13-14): hence, the other gospels would have been perverted. However, Galatians 2 does not deal with a difference in doctrine, but with a difference of behaviour. Besides, if it was true that later pseudo-apostles had perverted the other texts, then where are the originals? Is Marcion's edition authentic? Our gospel (Luke in its entirety) is older. Should our gospel be rejected as a perversion by comparing it with an edition that is of later origin?

IV 4: The age of the Gospel is decisive. Marcion does not appear on the scene until a full century after the publication of the great deeds and reports of the Christian religion. A letter exists, written before the time of his apostasy, which shows that Marcion had earlier accepted the whole gospel of Luke. Marcion is unable to produce an older version of his work. Hence, he is the one who brings something new.

IV 5: In order to determine the age of the gospel we need to go to the (mother) churches. When we do so, it is evident that the earliest churches all possessed a complete gospel of Luke. True, Marcion also has churches within his orbit that use his version of Luke, but these are younger churches that he has set up himself. Apparently, even a wasp makes nests! Since the more ancient churches also had other gospels, Marcion will have to edit them too. Either that, or else some of his followers will have to do it for him.

IV 5,7: Conclusion: The argument against the heretics has two parts: in chronological order, the truth *came before* the lie, and the *concordant authority* of the early church as a whole demonstrates what the church holds to be old and apostolic.

The New Testament canon: closed in the fourth century?

The response of the writers of the church to Marcion's efforts shows that there must have been some kind of New Testament canon *before* this 'mutilator of the Bible' set to work. The body that Marcion meant to dissect was older than the surgeon. His self-willed canon could be characterized as a *reduction* of the New Testament Scriptures.

However, was this New Testament already fully complete before Marcion, or was it still, in spite of its recognizable unity, not quite closed during the 2nd century? This question deserves separate attention. There is a widespread view that the limits of the New Testament were not fully fixed until the 3rd or 4th centuries. Not only was the canon not definitively closed, so goes the claim, but it was not until this later period that a definite decision was made to include a number of smaller and still disputed texts.[29] The *idea* of a canon might well have predated Marcion, but its actual completion would not have taken place till after him, and might in fact have been promoted by the challenges he had posed.

The most widely quoted sources in support of this claim (that the establishment of the New Testament canon as we know it dates from the 3rd and 4th centuries AD) are the 39th Festal (Easter) Letter of Athanasius, and a declaration by the Synod of Carthage. We will discuss each of these in what follows.

Athanasius

According to many scholars, the exact extent of the New Testament (at least around its margins) was still in dispute in the days of Eusebius and Origen. It was Athanasius of Alexandria who used his ecclesiastical authority to impose a final solution in the second half of the 4th century. Wikenhauser Schmid's *Handbook* reads: *"At its earliest, the canon was closed in its final form in Egypt, by means of the 39th Paschal Letter of Patriarch Athanasius on Alexandria in 367"*.[30]

This seems to be a surprising turn of events: one man, with a stroke of the pen in 367 AD, succeeded in bringing an end to doubts from which the church had been suffering for centuries!

We are even asked to believe that on this point his great opponents, the followers of Arius, had submitted to Athanasius' authority, for there is no evidence of any disagreement between the Arian and the orthodox views about the extent of the New Testament. It seems worthwhile to examine this letter, which is said to have had such a unifying effect, more closely.

In Athanasius' letter we do indeed find a list of the 27 books of the New Testament as we know them. After providing his list, Athanasius continues: *"These are fountains of salvation, that they who thirst may be satisfied with the living words they contain. In these alone is proclaimed the doctrine of godliness"*.[31]

It is this final phrase that should make us think. Modern works tell us that Athanasius *drew* the boundaries of the canon, while this passage rather creates the impression that he *defended* them. It is as if he wished to resist the advance of other texts by saying that the truth is to be found *"in these alone"*. What was Athanasius' aim? Was it to impose a decision on the canonicity of the books that he had included in his list? Or is he more concerned about the defence of these (already acknowledged) books against a new danger?

Anyone who reads the letter as a whole will discover soon enough what Athanasius' purpose for this listing of the canon is. He is not taking definitive decisions about what should or should not be included in the canon; rather, he is concerned about what ought *not* to be allowed to intrude into the canon, because it never belonged. In his days, Christians were at risk of being drawn away from simple devotion to God (he quotes II Corinthians 2:11), and of succumbing to other, apocryphal books instead. In name, they appear to resemble the 'true books'. Just as Luke 'carefully investigated' to confirm the truth of history, (Luke 1:1-4), so Athanasius aims to confirm the truth of the Bible against the later competition of heretical and non-apostolic writings:

> *"Forasmuch as some have taken in hand to reduce into order for themselves the books termed apocryphal, and to mix them up with the divinely inspired Scripture, concerning which we have been fully persuaded, as they who from the beginning were eyewitnesses and ministers of the Word, delivered to the fathers; it seemed good to me also, having been urged thereto by true brethren, and having learned from the beginning, to set before you the books included in the Canon, and handed down, and accredited as Divine; to the end that anyone who has fallen into error may condemn those who have led him astray; and that he who has continued steadfast in purity may again rejoice, having these things brought to his remembrance".*

This introduction shows us clearly that it was not at all Athanasius' intention to force a decision on disputed matters. Rather, he sees himself, as leader of the church, compelled to defend the long-accepted books from being mixed with all kinds of apocryphal encroachments, and he does so by reminding them of what has been passed on from of old as having divine authority. The church is called to *hold fast* to these divine Scriptures.

Athanasius did not write this Easter letter of 367 with the intention of resolving any possible remaining doubts about the extent of the New Testament. This is also evident from the fact that he begins by listing the books of the *Old* Testament. In doing so, he follows the canon of the Hebrew Bible, and he leaves out altogether the so-called apocryphal or deuterocanonical books that were included in the Greek Bible.

After listing the 27 books of the New Testament, he repeats what he said earlier about his purpose for writing. By listing the canonical books, he aims to clearly show which later, fictional texts have never belonged. For these heretical fabrications, which have the appearance of ancient texts, he uses the term 'apocrypha'; for him, 'apocryphal' has a different meaning than it did in later periods. This becomes obvious when, next to what Athanasius calls "canonical and apocryphal" books (by which he means: heretical, of later invention), he also introduces a group of books of which he says that while they do not belong to the canon (not *kanonizomena*), they were received by the fathers as being suitable for reading to catechumens. These are the books that *we* now refer to as 'apocrypha'. As examples, he lists books that date from the Old Testament period, such as the *Wisdom of Solomon*, the *Wisdom of Sirach*, *Esther*, *Judith*, and *Tobit*, as well as books that had always been valued as literature of the New Covenant, such as the *Didache* and Hermas' *The Shepherd*. Athanasius lists these books, not because he wants to distance them from the canon, but because he wants to ensure that his sharp condemnation of the 'apocryphal books' does not extend to these valuable non-canonical writings. *"…The former, my brethren, are included in the Canon, the latter being [merely] read; nor is there in any place a mention of apocryphal writings. But they are an invention of heretics, who write them when they choose, bestowing upon them their approbation, and assigning to them a date, that so, using them as ancient writings, they may find occasion to lead astray the simple"*.

Our conclusion is that Athanasius' Paschal letter recognizes that the canon as we know it is an established and ancient point of departure in dealing with the intrusions of pseudo-ancient and heretical apocrypha. This letter cannot be characterized as an authoritative statement intended to remove doubts about the canonicity of certain Bible books. Athanasius' letter deserves a place in church history, as a document in the struggle for the *preservation* of the pure canon, but not as part of the history of the *establishment* of the canon itself. It cannot be regarded as a document that informs the shaping or the closing of the canon, even though this might have become a widely held view in the 19th and 20th centuries.

The Council of Carthage

The currently prevailing view among contemporary scholars is that Athanasius' decision in relation to a number of disputed Bible books received a seal of approval in the declarations of later ecclesiastical councils.

Kümmel writes: "*There can be no doubt that not only Augustine (influenced by Jerome) supported Athanasius' canon, but also that the African Council of Hippo Regius (of 393), established the same extent of the canon*".[32] In this view, the ship of the canon, adrift for centuries on the sea of history, has finally found a place to anchor. At least, that is how it seems, when the declaration of Hippo Regius is confirmed at the Council of Carthage in 397AD. The Acts of this Council have recorded the text of this decision for us.[33]

When we consult these Acts, we find a list of books containing not only the New, but also the Old Testament. This would be somewhat surprising if their intent was to make a definitive decision concerning the last disputed books of the *New* Testament. The heading of the list, however, puts us on the right track:

> *Canon 24:* "*That besides the Canonical Scriptures nothing be read in church under the name of divine Scripture. … the Canonical Scriptures are as follows …*":

From this heading it is evident that the 'canonical Scriptures' are already a known entity. At issue here is not the *limits* of these writings, but the agreement that from now on the so-called 'reading of Scripture' in the church services should no longer include other edifying works. From now on, only the canonical books deserve a place as Scripture readings in the worship services. From Athanasius' Paschal Letter we know that before this moment the *Didache* and *Hermas* were sometimes read in church. In his *De Viris Illustribus*, Jerome too points out that there are still Greek churches in which *Hermas* is sometimes included in the readings in church.[34] The Council of Carthage deemed it desirable to *limit* the liturgical readings to the canonical books. In order to facilitate this regulation, the list of books is attached: infractions can now be easily determined. Any book that is not included in the canon *as specified here* may no longer be considered eligible for reading aloud in worship.

The declaration of Carthage has been wrongly given a place in the history of the canon. After all, it is not directed to the demarcation or closing of the canon. This declaration deserves a place in the history of *liturgy*: it regulates the *use* of the canon in worship, and it marks the end of a period in which next to the canonical books other ancient edifying texts were read in the churches. Just as Athanasius took his starting point in a long-established canon, so the Councils near the end of the 4th century AD proceeded from a canon that was already beyond dispute.

Conclusion

The period of the 3rd and 4th centuries AD has no separate significance in relation to the delineation or the recognition of the canon. It is clear, however, that in this period the rise of pseudo-ancient heretical texts posed a threat to the established canon, and that to counter this threat the canon received a position of monopoly in the liturgical readings. Only the Book of Revelation was still subject to attempts to have it removed from the canon: these attempts, however, did not arise because the canon might not have been closed yet; rather, they owed their origin to objections that were nursed against the use or abuse of its contents.

To ascertain the time in which the canon of the New Testament was established, we must go back further than the 3rd or 4th centuries. Further back, even, than the period before Marcion. What had been accepted as Scripture from the earliest beginnings of the church, and passed on since then, had been challenged (Marcion; Revelation) or threatened (heretical pseudo-literature), but its essence was not shaped or developed in the centuries that followed. What had from of old been accepted and applied in the church did not need a later demarcation; what it did need was continuing protection.

The Bible follows in God's footsteps

In the previous sections of this chapter we have investigated whether there is any truth to the claim that the canon arose from selection processes within the church, and that the canon actually derives its authority from those processes. It turns out that this contention is historically incorrect. The church did not produce lists of writings in order to elevate some of them (and not others) to the dignified level of 'Bible books'; rather, it gathered lists of books to determine which of them had already been accepted from the earliest times as authoritative by all the churches. The formal listing of the canon sealed their already functioning authority.

The question still remains, however: how did the canonical books gain this recognition? The question concerning the authority of the canon is not yet answered when currently prevailing answers are shown to be insufficient. In fact, this only heightens the urgency of the question. If we were dealing with a book which in its totality had originated from *one* period, or was written by *one* person, its authority could easily be explained by respect for the stature of its author or the time of its origin. That is the case with the book of Islam: the Koran is completely the book of Mohammed. Anyone who accepts that Mohammed is the prophet of Allah will have no difficulty with the authority of the Koran.

The Bible, however, is an entirely different kind of book: it incorporates texts from various time periods and a great variety of authors. Nor are we dealing with a book that has been found somewhere, that inspires awe through its mysterious appearance, such as, for instance, the Book of Mormon. Instead, the Bible has *grown*, and much of this growth has been quiet and unobtrusive. We can see a tree, with all its branches, twigs and leaves, but no-one has been able to mark its growth with the aid of significant events. Of all the books in the world, the history of the Bible's origins extends across the greatest length of time (roughly one-and-a-half millennia). It is precisely the span of time of its development that makes the questions concerning its age, its origins and the authority of its canon so urgent. In the course of the many centuries encompassing the history of the origin of the Scriptures, there have been numerous others who produced other books with similar pretensions. There were so many other prophets than just Micaiah the son of Imlah who spoke in the name of the LORD: who decided which of them were false prophets, and who was the true prophet? There were so many pious and religious texts in circulation: how did people know that Solomon's *Book of Wisdom* and the *Letter of Barnabas* ought not to be accepted as canonical writings?

If the canon was not the product of the church, how did it find its way into the church without anyone noticing? To find the answer to this question, we must take a different approach from what we usually do. We are accustomed to look backwards through the centuries, to try to discern what took place before the time of the established canon. People search out the prehistory of the canon and approach it from this direction. However, we must approach it from the other side, not by starting with the canon, and tracing tracing it backwards to the various books of the Bible, but by starting with the period *before* the Bible books and moving forward towards the canon. It is only from this point of departure that we will discover the contours of the mystery that today we call 'canon'.

God's own appearance precedes the Scriptures

As people created by God, we did not begin in this world with pieces of paper about God. In Paradise, he sought us out, in the cool of the evening, to speak with us personally. There was no need for pen and paper: there was direct contact, a face-to-face communion (Genesis 2:16, 3:8-9). Even after the fall into sin, God let himself be heard without the mediation of a third party (Genesis 4:9-16; 6:13ff). Abram receives a direct command, and more than once God speaks confidentially to him, as to a friend (Genesis 12:1ff; 18:17ff). It is not impossible that during these centuries some of the words of God, and some of the associated events were recorded in writing. But still, our written canon does not begin with Enoch or Abram, but with Moses.

The Lord appeared very personally to Moses. God says this very clearly to Aaron and Miriam: *"If there is a prophet among you, I the Lord make myself known to him in a vision; I speak with him in a dream. Not so with my servant Moses. He is faithful in all my house. With him I speak mouth to mouth, clearly, and not in riddles, and he beholds the form of the Lord"* (Numbers 12:6-8). The Lord authorized Moses by the deeds he was able to perform. Moses was enabled to call forth the ten dreadful plagues upon Egypt, events that centuries later still made the Philistines quake with fear (I Samuel 4:8). Moses was allowed to open the waters of the Red Sea for the people of Israel, and close them again over the heads of Pharaoh's pursuing army. Unimaginable events took place. Even the hard-as-stone Pharaoh had to bow to them. They were supernatural facts. And in the middle of all these divine acts stood one man: Moses. He was the only one to be allowed to climb Mount Sinai, shrouded in fire and smoke: no other person could approach this awe-inspiring holiness. It is Moses who hears the ten words of the covenant, and comes down to bring them to the people. Now, to believe in Yahweh is to listen to Moses. Everyone acknowledges that God has authorized Moses. At this moment, with the column of cloud and fire in the camp, and with the voice of God thundering from the mountain, that is impossible to deny. That is also why we read: *"so the people feared the Lord, and they believed in the Lord and in his servant Moses"* (Exodus 14:31).

This awe for God's appearance and great works, and hence for the man who is God's trusted servant, will naturally incorporate respect for the written record of God's words and Moses' commands. To a significant degree, Moses himself, a first-class scholar in Pharaoh's palace, took charge of creating this written record. More than once, God explicitly commanded him to *"write this on a scroll"* (Exodus 17:14, 24:4), and Moses himself commends his written legacy to the people as the means to find the way of life with God (Deuteronomy 28:58, 31:24-29). The Book of the Law was placed next to the Ark of the Covenant (Deuteronomy 31:26). In the ark had been placed the stone tablets, on which the Lord himself had inscribed the Ten Words. That is also why the ark had been called 'the ark of the testimony'. The proclamation of the covenant, given to Moses, was kept here. The glory of the Lord, descending in the cloud, sanctified first the tabernacle, and then the temple of Solomon: everyone could see that the Living God lent his authority to the house that was anchored in the Law of Moses (Exodus 40:34-38; I Kings 8:10-11).

The mystery of Moses' canon is this: before Moses wrote, the Lord himself appeared in a manner that was unmistakable. People could place their confidence in later leaders only to the extent that these leaders reflected the radiance of this man of God. Hence, we read about Joshua, Moses' successor:

> *"And Joshua the son of Nun was full of the spirit of wisdom, for Moses had laid his hands on him. So the people of Israel obeyed him and did as the Lord had commanded Moses. And there has not arisen a prophet since in Israel like Moses, whom the Lord knew face to face, none like him for all the signs and the wonders that the Lord sent him to do in the land of Egypt, to Pharaoh and to all his servants and to all his land, and for all the mighty power and all the great deeds of terror that Moses did in the sight of all Israel"* (Deuteronomy 34:9-12).

Moses sets the standard for the whole Old Testament period. Through him, the Lord had also indicated how prophets could be distinguished, true from false. God provided two criteria, both of which were an extension of his revelation through Moses:

1. The prophecy must come true: there has to be evidence that the prophet has not spoken presumptuously, but that the Lord (who performs great deeds and knows the future) has put his words in the prophet's mouth (Deuteronomy 18:21-22).

2. The prophecy may not entice the people to turn away from Moses' commandments: in such cases the signs and wonders performed by the prophets are misleading messages from the devil (Deuteronomy 13:1-5).

It is not so that that the people of Israel established criteria after the fact, in order to select from the great variety of prophecies what was truly the Word of God; rather, these criteria to test each word of prophecy had been provided beforehand. The streambed of canonical writing was there already beforehand, and not dug afterwards to channel the flow of the river.

After Moses, the Spirit of the LORD does not fall silent. He fills the hearts of judges and directs the hearts of kings. This leads to deeds that are worthy of being kept in memory, and to words that must be held in honour. The inspired works of the wild and weak-hearted Samson show that the grace of God for Israel continues to break through, even through a person who had so little direction in his own life. When David reunites the people around the ark of God's testimony, this is the outcome of the LORD's leading and anointing. In the Psalms, the king becomes a prophet. Israel gets to hear more than they did during their wilderness journey, but none of it is a departure from what they had heard earlier. It is precisely because all of this moves within the framework of Moses' norms that it is worth remembering and worth keeping.

Solomon's words have authority in that God gave him such exceptional wisdom that people came to hear him from as far away as Africa. A recognition of this divine gift leads to respect for its fruits in Solomon's own writings. The laws of Moses are applied in concrete settings in the Proverbs, and take on colourful hues in the Song of Songs.

We see another, similar authorization of prophets who follow Moses' line, and who take a stand for the commandments that were given by way of Moses, when fire comes down from heaven on Mount Carmel. Even Ahab himself is shaken to the core by that event. And by the signs and wonders that Elijah performs, Israel is reminded of the wondrous acts of God, through Moses, in Egypt and in the wilderness. The accounts that tell about kings and prophets, written by the prophets themselves, or recounted in other prophetic writings (II Chronicles 9:29; 12:15; 20:34; 32:32) need not be given a tailwind, so to speak, by a process of canonization. They already have the wind in their sails because they are obviously driven along by the same tempest that blew around Mount Sinai.

Powerfully driven are also the activities of the last Old Testament prophet: John the Baptist. Multitudes come flocking to his baptism, inspired as he is by the spirit of Elijah, and because in him the age-old promises are nearing fulfilment.

Then comes the moment when Moses is finally overshadowed. However, Moses himself had foretold that this would happen. Later, Someone would come, Someone to whom everyone must listen, having listened to Moses himself first. On the mountain, the LORD had not wanted his people to come up to meet him. That is why they had to settle for Moses, the mediator. Still, a personal encounter between the LORD and his people would one day become a reality. That would happen when the LORD would come to them in the form of a prophet, a second and better Moses. In Deuteronomy 18:15-19 we read:

> *"The LORD your God will raise up for you a prophet like me from among you, from your brothers — it is to him you shall listen – just as you desired of the LORD your God at Horeb on the day of the assembly, when you said, 'Let me not hear again the voice of the LORD my God or see this great fire any more, lest I die.' And the LORD said to me, 'They are right in what they have spoken. I will raise up for them a prophet like you from among their brothers. And I will put my words in his mouth, and he shall speak to them all that I command him. And whoever will not listen to my words that he shall speak in my name, I myself will require it of him."*

This will be no ordinary prophet; rather, he is the one who overcomes the objection that no one can meet the LORD in his great fire. Later, following on from the mediator Moses, this great representative Jesus will come. In regard to him, there is no question of his having to abide by what Moses had said. He carries the authority of Yahweh in himself. He is the Great Prophet, the definitive one.

That is how Jesus is proclaimed by John the Baptist, and that is how he teaches, with authority, to the amazement of the crowds (Matthew 7:28,29). The signs that he does prove that he has come from the Father. He does the Father's works, and these works authenticate him (John 10:38). In the words of the apostle Peter, Jesus of Nazareth *"was sent to you by God, and attested to you by God with mighty works and wonders and signs that God did through him in your midst, as you yourselves know"* (Acts 2:22). The apostle John testifies: *"And the Word became flesh and dwelt among us, and we have seen his glory, glory as of the only Son from the Father, full of grace and truth"* (John 1:14). It is the evidence of God's appearing in Jesus Christ that lends authority to the books that reflect his glory in their accounts.

The reality of Jesus the Christ also becomes clear in the outpouring of the Holy Spirit, and in the gifts that accompany his coming. Even before a pen is put to paper for the writing of the New Testament, tongues were baptized in the Holy Spirit, and healing hands were laid on the sick. By these signs, the Lord confirmed the message that the apostles brought about him, and it is in the light of this authorization that the New Testament letters were written.

We have barely touched on a few key moments. These, however, sufficiently show that the authority of the canon did not follow along *behind* the books of the New Testament, but that the authority of the great works of God actually went *before* them. The mystery of the Bible lies in the manifestations of the Lord, in fire and in the flesh. Without faith in these manifestations, in these works and words, it is hard for us to come to any understanding about the authority of the canon. With that faith, however, the canon becomes much more for us than simply a sacred codex: it has become the burning bush, in which we have come to stand before the LORD God himself. We need not kneel before a desert shrub or sustainably-sourced paper, but together with his people we must bow before the God of Mount Sinai, who manifests himself here, and whose voice we hear. We must bow before his Son, together with all the apostles.

The awe-inspiring authority of the canon has not been derived after the fact from various councils, but from the awesome and unexpected deeds of the Triune God in the world. It is through the Scriptures that we see the glory of the LORD (II Corinthians 3). And that is why the Scriptures have now been sanctified as *Holy* Scriptures.

God's own words appoint the authors of the Scriptures

The authority of God's own appearing is the root of the authority of the Scriptures. This fundamental consideration, however, has not yet brought us to the last word. For the question remains: why haven't *all* the writings that move in the line of Moses been incorporated in the Scriptures? And why have other texts, which also stand in the apostolic tradition, not been assigned an ecclesiastical status? Might it be that while the *authority* of the canon does not rest on ecclesiastical decisions, perhaps the *extent* of the canon does? In that case, could there still be room to discuss whether it might be desirable to as yet include the Apocrypha, books such as the *Wisdom of Solomon*, in the canon? Or to consider whether a book such as Hermas' *The Shepherd* might not be honourably reinstated in our liturgy?

Over against this line of thinking we may note that the LORD himself, by means of his revelation, has indicated which of his servants would serve as bearers of his revelation, and as authors of the sacred Scriptures. The books of Moses proceed from the assumption that prophets and seers receive direct (though possibly veiled) revelations from God. When their words come true, their audience must *keep on* listening. The Old Testament does not often indicate explicitly that a certain person has the gift of prophecy. And yet, it is clear that David (to mention just one example) is to be regarded as a prophet (Acts 2:30).

Not every edifying word needs to be held in such esteem, but the words that the Lord newly proclaims by way of his prophets and the inspired poets should be so honoured.

No prophet arose in the period between Malachi and John the Baptist. Edifying and largely reliable books were written during this period, comparable in many respects to the earlier prophetic writings. Since they were not the product of a new and direct revelation, however, they were not given a place in the Jewish Bible. The apocrypha found a home in the Greek tradition of Jewish literature (the Septuagint), and this often left Christian readers with the impression that these apocryphal books had authority that was equal to the canon itself. The criterion to include or exclude these books is not whether they were ortho- or heterodox. Instead, what was decisive was that these texts date from a time when the source of prophecy had run dry. When the flow resumes, as it does with John the Baptist, the record of such prophecy resumes as well.

In the New Testament, we note that the Lord Jesus entrusts his disciples, those who were with him up to the end of his sojourn on earth, and who after Pentecost were to serve him as apostles and elders, with a special task in relation to binding or loosing (Matthew 16:19; 18:18). Space does not permit us here to explore the great significance of this divine authority.[35] However, it is important to note that Jesus himself gave a special qualification to the apostles and elders, as men of the first hour, as men also who were themselves authenticated through signs and wonders, to have authority over succeeding generations. This authority sets a boundary for the origin of authoritative texts for succeeding generations. It limits the scope for the creation of the church's authoritative Scriptures to the first generation. Whatever might appear after this time in the way of edifying literature lacks the authorization of the Lord himself. It must conform to the standard of the writings of the prophets and the apostles: these are the foundation on which the church is built. It is the words and commands of the prophets and apostles that form the church's foundation (Ephesians 2:20). It is not so that at a certain moment the church called a halt to the extension of the canon. Rather, it was the Lord himself who limited the number of his prophets; sometimes he sent no prophets at all. He is the same one who found it sufficient to lend his divine authority to the generation of the apostles and the elders.

God's own guidance filled the hands of the church.

It is not only the *authority* of the canon that rests in the initiative of God, in his manifestation. The *limits* of the canon, too, are derived from the historical contours that God himself has interposed in his revelation and his authoritative speaking. Of course, this is decisive, but still there is more to be said. When we approach the Bible as it presently lies before us, a number of questions about its details remain. Several of these questions are presently beyond our ability to resolve (example: do the books of Samuel have their origins in the schools of the prophets, or were they compiled by one prophet only?). Other questions relate to specific Bible books, and they can only be considered as part of a broader introduction to each specific book.

However, there is also a question of a more general nature that must still be discussed in connection with the canon. Why have all kinds of *other* prophetic and apostolic texts been lost for posterity, and why is it especially *these* texts that have been preserved?

In our opinion, it would not be correct to speak of an intentional architectural design of the Bible. As if the Bible is a building that can be regarded as complete because it conforms precisely to *this* structure, and where all other remaining building materials could be discarded. Just because we do not have all of Solomon's songs does not mean that the missing ones failed to meet God's standard. Just because we have lost track of certain letters from Paul to Laodicea and Corinth does not necessarily mean that these letters must have been of lesser quality. Evidently not everything that was spoken with divine authority has actually been preserved for us. The Bible is an anthology, a selection, not an exhaustive archive. It was compiled for the sake of our salvation, not as a museum that contains every holy Scripture that was ever written.

It isn't possible for us to determine whether there might have been holy Scriptures that were lost to us through human carelessness or deliberate intent. If that were so, we would have a Bible that, because of the church's fault, is more limited than it could have been. However, we can be certain that God, who appeared on Mount Sinai, and who by his Spirit preserves his church, has never allowed his church to be robbed of the essential parts of Scripture. While we may not know if there could have been more, we can be certain that in any case it was *enough*. The only thing that we can do is to scrupulously pass on those Scriptures that *have* been preserved.

According to some, the Bible is quite intentionally no larger and no smaller than it actually is. We ought actually to be pleased that we no longer have Paul's letter to Laodicea: the Bible has been so tailored as to conform perfectly to its design. Such a thought, however, is open to objection. Nowhere in the Bible do we find any indication that the Lord intended to provide a precise composition for the Bible. On the contrary, there is a certain degree of superfluity to the Scriptures that make it hard to regard it as an ordered legal codex, in which every sentence fits exactly like a brick in a wall. This has to do with the generosity of God and the obstinate unwillingness of the hearers. *"Long ago, God spoke to our fathers at many times and in many ways by the prophets"* (Hebrews 1:1), and Paul is not ashamed, for the benefit of the congregation, to write the same things more than once. (Philippians 3:1; II Thessalonians 3:10; II Corinthians 13:2). Prophets such as Ezekiel and Jeremiah had to repeat and portray the same message over and over again, to impress upon the people the need for repentance.

There is a degree of redundancy in what the Bible says. It is functional. It causes the word of God to come to us at all levels, and ensures that we do not depend for clear understanding on one single text. The Bible's beneficial superfluity keeps us from thinking that our salvation should depend on every last letter. And it ensures that the Bible will never be too limited to serve through many centuries and among many peoples. Its storehouses are so full that not every reader will need everything in them at the same time. A missionary in Africa will be able to put Moses' ceremonial laws to greater use than a minister in the Netherlands. And a poet is more likely to be edified by the poetic pieces of Scripture than someone who is less emotionally attuned.

Returning now to the question: why have *these* texts been preserved within the bounds of the canon, and not others? The only answer we can give is that through God's care it is in any case not too little, and that for the church it will always be enough.

When believers neared the time of the end of the Old Covenant, and took stock of all their treasures, they found that they possessed the Law, the Prophets and the Writings. When the church, in its first centuries, began to order its authentic documents, it came no further than what we have now. Since it is certain that some of the texts of the prophets and apostles have been lost to us, it is no wonder that the church is careful to preserve what it has been left with. Since God has filled our hands, we are to take care not to let anything fall. That is why the church uses the confessions to count on its fingers, as it were, what its hands have been filled with. And that is also why the whole Bible has been gathered and bound into one volume that we call *the Bible*.

Here, we encounter a marvellous paradox. For centuries, the church has lived from the Scriptures. In our times, there are widespread calls for a re-evaluation of the canon, of its nature and of its authority. If these calls were to arise from reverence for the living God of Mount Sinai, then it seems that one would want in any case to hold onto what we already have. In practice, however, it appears that the texts of the Scriptures are being left to fall to the ground, left and right, as a cobbled-together collection of merely human documents. Is this evidence of reverence for God, or is this fashionable disputation about the origin of the canon little more than a smokescreen? Is the history of the origin of the Bible being cloaked in mist, because its decisive prior history, that of God's manifestation and his great works, has been lost from sight?

Our respect for the age and the authority of the canon is as great as our reverence for God's manifestation in our flesh is deep.

CHAPTER 2

The enduring value of the Bible

Is there still any point to reading the Bible in the 21st century? The Bible is a collection of all kinds of texts from a distant past: isn't it well and truly past its use-by date?

This question presents itself to us in different forms:

1. Don't we live in a completely different time, and isn't the Bible a culture-bound book from a bygone age?
2. Hasn't science overtaken the Bible, and hasn't our present understanding of the world rendered its worldview obsolete?
3. Wouldn't it be better to limit ourselves to the residual value of the Bible, a value that is to be found chiefly in the ancient authors' *purpose* in writing those time-bound texts?

Answers to these questions will strongly determine the readers' attitudes to what they read. That is why we cannot sidestep them as we open the Bible in the 21st century.

Different times

The view that the Bible is a time-bound product of bygone generations is by now widespread. Consequently, many readers of this Bible expect little more than outdated statements of faith that are difficult to uphold in our day and age. This is the case in spite of the fact that the Bible itself, on almost every page, clearly aims to transcend the times in which its authors lived, and claims to have purpose and meaning that extends to the end of time. The low expectations of modern readers do not connect well with the high aim of the text that lies before them.

Why is it so difficult for many of today's readers to find enduring meaning in the Scriptures? Because these readers of the Bible generally hold to a fairly unique proposition: texts from earlier times are automatically time-bound and as such have lesser value. This is not a proposition that can be easily upheld in general. It certainly does not apply when we read the works of Plato, Confucius or Karl Marx. It is normal that we first let the texts speak for themselves, and then consider whether or not they transcend their time of origin. We do this because we take for granted that there have been certain people whose thinking retains universal significance, even if what they wrote bears traces of the time in which it was written. Why should we suddenly lose this confidence when we read the Bible? After all, we discover in the Bible that Jesus Christ didn't limit himself to the spiritual care of his contemporaries; on the contrary, he said and did a great deal that was *meant* to have universal and enduring significance, a great deal that even today serves for Christians as a valuable guide.

Unbelievers may evaluate this claim of significance, and choose not to accept it for themselves, labelling what Jesus said as 'outdated'. But imposing such a value judgement concerning the contents of the text as a hermeneutical presupposition upon the *reading* of the text is inconsistent with any kind of scholarly integrity or validity, as if it is *a priori* certain that the contents of this book *must* be largely outdated simply because the Bible is an ancient book.

It is certainly true that there is much that is noteworthy in the Bible because of its time of origin. If nothing else, we see that in the languages it uses. Of course, there is much more: its relationship with daily life in ancient times, its connections with ancient history, its points of contact with ancient cultures and religions. The Bible is not a timeless book, a collection of merely graphic symbols removed from any relationship with language.

This implies that present-day readers of the Bible will need some help. They are no longer familiar with the language or the time of the Bible, and are therefore less able to fully comprehend the context in which the text is embedded.

This does not imply that the Bible's meaning can only be unlocked by means of auxiliary fields of knowledge, such as archaeology, linguistics, or national and cultural history. But it does mean that we need these auxiliary disciplines to sharpen our view of what we read. Without such knowledge, the image becomes hazy, and misunderstandings are likely to arise. Those who have grown up in our Western culture will already have much of this prior knowledge at their disposal, but a mission church in Africa may have much less. These are degrees of difference, but still the neglect of these fields of knowledge will inevitably lead to a growing loss of clarity in our understanding.

However, these auxiliary disciplines cannot be used as tools to dismiss the text of the Bible as the 'product of a bygone era'. Instead, their value is to lend colour to the texts as spoken *in their time*.

There is more. Not only did the various parts of the Bible come into existence in their own distinct periods, they also possess a historical context that relates to their place within the progressive history of revelation. This history of revelation (*'historia revelationis'*) is the closest and most significant historical context for the various parts of the Bible. Events from the history of Germany must of course be placed against the backdrop of the history of Europe, but they must first of all be viewed within the framework of *German* history. Likewise, passages from the Bible should of course be placed within the framework of their own time, but first of all they must be framed by the history of God's revelation.

For example: since in the Old Testament adultery was punishable by death, it is helpful to find out how adultery was punished in the nations that surrounded Israel. That helps us assess whether the original readers of the Old Testament text regarded the prescribed penalty as severe, lenient or simply as matter-of-fact.

However, it is even more important to examine this punishment in the light of what God had earlier said, already in Paradise, about the institution of marriage: "*A man ... will hold fast to his wife*" (Gen 2:24). This word from Genesis is the primary determinant for the penalty against adultery *in Israel*. We should also remember that in the Exodus from Egypt, God forged Israel into a unified people with its own system of laws. This situation explains the form of the *penal sanction*, namely the death penalty.

It may be that the existing laws of Egypt and Assyria might throw some more light on whether or not the *severity* of the punishment was unusual.

The fact that in the New Covenant era adulterers within the Christian church were not stoned is not because of the so-called 'time-bound' character of penal sanctions in the Bible; rather, it has to do with the progress of God's revelation, from a church gathered in one nation in the Old Testament, to a church gathered from all nations in the New. The church in Israel had a role, on behalf of God, in administering civil laws; the New Testament church no longer has such a role. In all of this, the enduring meaning of the Old Testament penal code remains before the God of Paradise, an adulterer is liable to the death penalty. Hence, we read in the Book of Revelation that "*outside are … the sexually immoral and murderers and idolaters*" (Revelations 22:15). It is only through Jesus' *death* that there is acquittal and life for adulterers who repent and believe.

One frequently used example relates to Paul's instructions to slaves. Wasn't it time-bound circumstance that led the apostle to urge slaves to submit to their masters? And then in the same breath the conclusion follows: in the same way, Paul's statements about husband-and-wife relationships are time-bound. This conclusion overlooks, however, that Paul's statements about marriage are rooted in Creation and in the story of the Fall, while there is no such justification in regard to slavery. Paul's commands to slaves are placed within existing and time-bound relationships.

Still, even in this case there is more to be said. Paul speaks from an Old Testament context where – within Israel – slavery had already been abolished, and he speaks to slave owners in a manner that puts a bomb under any kind of exploitation of existing master-slave relationships. Paul's letter to Philemon is instructive in this respect: he asks Christian slave owners to consider setting their slaves free, and at the very least he expects owners to regard their slaves as brothers. We quite rightly do not see Paul's instructions in this matter as a command to *have* slaves. Still, even with the elimination of slavery, Paul's time-bound statements have not become outdated. The apostle commanded slaves to submit, not because that was their only means of survival in their situation, but because their new relationship to God in heaven also casts a new light on their labour relations on earth. By analogy, Paul's instruction still applies to relationships between employers and employees today.

A third example relates to the Sabbath command. The command to rest from labour on the Sabbath day had a ceremonial dimension, one that was superseded when the Saviour, resting in the grave, completed this seventh-day rest. However, the Sabbath command retains an enduring character now that the Saviour has set apart the first day of the week as a day of meeting, fellowship and worship. It is therefore hard to imagine that a day of rest for man and animal should have been abolished on the day of Easter. The day might shift, but the idea on which it is based remains. The rapidly declining honouring of the Sunday as a day of rest in a 24-hour economy, and the increasing acceptance of this trend, can only be seen as a wrong development. The Sunday still retains its function as a point of reference, directing us to the coming Sabbath rest that remains for the people of God. Hebrews 4:9 prevents us from devaluing or neglecting that aspect of rest in the weekly day of worship, or from dismissing it as an Old Testament and therefore outdated idea.

Through patient and careful reading, the exegete must ascertain, every time again, which elements of a passage are determined by their time, and which are universally valid. He inflicts a kind of textual blindness on himself, however, if he assumes *a priori* that 'another time' will render everything in the Bible time-bound and out-of-date.

A different view of the world

Many 21st century readers of the Bible feel that the Bible proceeds from an obsolete view of the world (one with an upper- and an underworld: heaven and hell). Since the contents of the Bible are closely interwoven with this view of the world, it may seem that many parts of the Bible are past their use-by date.

Of course, we ought to be careful not to ask too much of many Biblical expressions, as if they were scientific statements about a view of the world. Just as anyone would do today, the texts of the Bible often use the language of direct observation. We too speak of the sun rising and setting, even when we live with a view of the world in which the earth revolves around the sun. In the same way, the Bible does not base its reference to a 'rising sun' on a (by now obsolete) scientific model, but on ordinary everyday human observation. Even in ancient times, a heliocentric model, comparable to our own, was by no means unknown. In the Hellenistic world two models coexisted, the geocentric and the heliocentric, side-by-side. Scripture chooses neither the one nor the other. The Bible uses the language of normal observation, universal for people everywhere. Where the Bible speaks of 'heaven' and 'hell', it does not do so because its authors were unable to see more than a flat earth between the sky above and the waters below. The Biblical message about God's heaven and outer darkness is not the fruit of a limited view of the world, but a serious message to all human beings, whatever their worldviews or cultures might be.

Is there then no conflict with what science has discovered since then? Does our modern view of the world not limit, in a certain sense, the range of possible meanings of what we read in the Bible today? To take a concrete example: is the creation story of Genesis 1 still credible?

As we seek answers to these questions, we must take care not to fall into absolute contrasts. It is certainly true that the possible meanings of a text are partially determined by extra-textual possibilities. When Paul sails from Miletus to Caesarea, we know that this must have taken longer than half a day. Whenever we read a text there will always be a continuous interaction with our knowledge of known, verifiable realities. There is, however, a limit: when the meaning of the text resists limitations imposed by everyday reality or scientific findings, then the text takes precedence. In normal situations, I can accept without further elaboration that a prophet would have eaten regularly during a period of forty days, for otherwise he would have died of starvation. However, when we read that Elijah travelled for forty days and forty nights in the strength of one meal, and when the text categorically states that he ate no other food (I Kings 19:8), it is not for us to say that the meaning of the text must be out-of-date because our present knowledge of biology conclusively shows that no-one can travel for 40 days and nights without any food. What we can say is that there must have been something extraordinary about that food, or that through it God worked an extraordinary effect in Elijah.

Whenever exegetes no longer have the openness to read something in a text that is completely unexpected, and to their scientific minds quite impossible, they have struck themselves with textual blindness.

The account of Joshua's battle, where the sun stood still above Gibeon, and the moon above Aijalon, could easily strike modern readers, who are accustomed to much that their forebears couldn't have dreamed of, as totally inconceivable. The implications of such a stoppage of the heavenly bodies are so huge that it is unthinkable that the world could ever resume its normal course. However, exegetes who now say that this only happened 'in a manner of speaking' simply do an injustice to the intent of the text of Joshua 10:12-14. They overestimate their own extra-textual knowledge when such knowledge begins to overpower the text as it stands. Unbelieving interpreters of Scripture are often well aware of that. And so, they explain what the book of Joshua meant to say, and then dismiss it with a shrug of their shoulders. They too overestimate their own sense of what's possible, but at least they do not stealthily insert this insight as an *a priori* condition into their hermeneutics.

Exegetes must always carefully examine to what degree the text permits closer limitation by extra-textual information. They must also, however, have an open eye for the moment when the text of the Bible will *not* permit such limitation; when on the contrary it unmasks as 'not universally valid' the material we might want to bring forward. It is good to wipe our glasses regularly as we read, but having said that, we should not put blinkers on.

Residual value

Questions concerning the enduring validity of the meaning of Biblical texts seem to become much simpler when we limit ourselves to preserving the *intention* of the Bible's authors. In that case, we could leave much of what the texts say for what it is, and only retain their core intent (often referred to as their 'scope').

Now the Bible, taken as a whole, undoubtedly has a 'scope': to magnify the honour of God through the salvation of sinners, and to teach them to live lives of holiness in this world. The Bible has not been given to us merely as some kind of encyclopaedia of information.

In the same way, each part of the Bible also has its own intention or scope. The *point* of the story of David and Goliath is that the Lord saves by faith alone, not what giants looked like in ancient times.

Unfortunately however, this concept of 'scope' has been used far too often to dismiss the rest of the text. It is as if the suggestion that human beings are chiefly kept alive by the beating of their hearts should justify cutting off their arms and legs. However, that is just what is done with the Bible.

It is often said: "The Bible is not a scientific text-book". That, of course, is certainly true. However, by reducing the Bible's character and intent to being a 'book of salvation', the disastrous conclusion is presented that the Bible cannot have any relevance at all to scientific knowledge.

In other settings, we would flinch from such a proposition. It would be like saying that pieces of private correspondence could not contribute decisive material when writing about the history of another part of the world. Or that an old travel journal could not incidentally provide medical science with information about the therapeutic effects of a certain plant. There is a great deal that floats by on the surface of a river! There is much in the Bible of which we might not say that it expresses its core meaning or intent, but it *does* add value, and it *is* true.

We cannot do without this added value. In the first place, in the exegesis of the text. If Goliath were not a giant, if there were no giants in that time, then the 'scope' of the story collapses. For what then is left of the power of our faith? In addition, these facts may also be indispensable for fields of study that are not directly related to the Bible.

Here, we need to be alert to two dangers. First, that our focus on the *scope* of the text blinds us for details of Scripture that may also be relevant for other fields of knowledge, such as linguistics (as in the Babylonian confusion of speech), anthropology (the existence of giants, the genealogy of Shem, Ham and Japheth), or historiography (the period before the great Flood), etc.

The second danger, however, is that we, in our desire for a comprehensive Christian model for one of these fields of study, lose sight of the scope of the passage, and begin, at certain subsidiary points, to ask too much of the text. Biblical psychology, geology, linguistics, etc cannot be constructed upon limited and more or less incidental material that is included in passages of the Bible. We do believe that this data from the Bible can exercise its authority, but then in a more *regulative* sense. In any branch of science or field of study, conclusions that conflict with what the Bible says will be in error, or at least subject to correction. Any geology that wants to base truth statements concerning the age of human history on its theoretical model, and in doing so comes into conflict with what the Bible says about the creation of heaven and earth in six days, and the creation of Adam and Eve as ancestors of all humanity, has gone too far in drawing absolute conclusions. For Christians, a warning light will come on, and they must determine where an error was made. It might not always be possible to identify such errors, and for the time being the claims of geology and the revelation of the Bible might have to remain standing, irreconcilably, next to each other. People are then faced with the choice of allowing the direction of their lives to be determined by scientific models that are subject to change, or governed by the revelation of Scripture.

This would be just as true in the field of politics and warfare. Consider this example: weapons of war will always carry within them the risk of killing innocent civilians or harming the environment. Now imagine the development of a weapon that is *designed* precisely for this purpose: to kill innocent people or destroy the environment. If someone, after an analysis of power relationships, were to make a moral statement that allowed the use of this weapon, that would be in clear conflict with what Scripture teaches about the powers of the civil authorities to punish evildoers and reward those who do right. Again, a warning light should come on. Of course, that is not the end of the matter. Waving a protest banner against nuclear, biological or chemical weapons is a simplistic and biblicistic response. Rather, we are called to a Biblical analysis: where have we gone wrong in our culture and view of warfare that we have so completely lost our way?

Exegetes must always and carefully establish the scope of the text, and the function of all its elements. Their view will be clouded, however, if they are only able to look through the lens of 'the scope of the text'. Such tunnel vision will frequently result in a total textual blindness. In our generation, readers, by limiting themselves to the scope of the text, have lost sight completely of anything else that there is to see in this 'book of yesterday'.

Enduring value for whom?

The first three sections of this chapter dealt primarily with whether the text *as such* is still worth keeping for later generations. We could, however, also approach the text from another perspective: *for whom* does the text of the Bible have enduring value? The usefulness and credibility of the text also have to do with the attitude of the reader. His or her interests and prejudices will often determine the personal response to the question whether these ancient texts "still have something to say".

This is true already as a general principle. Old texts about Chinese medicine will be seen as out of date and irrelevant for anyone who takes modern Western anatomy and physiology as their absolute starting point. On the other hand, adherents of alternative therapies often regard them as still valuable and useful. Serious students of the history of colonialism and the slave trade in the West Indies will find it hard to avoid a sense of guilt about abuses of the past, but a racist will be much more easily inclined to deny the impact of past practices.

What counts in general, counts even more when reading or studying the Bible. Christians are much more likely to search for enduring meanings in the Bible than Muslims would, or atheists. Still, there is one problem that confronts every reader. The things that Scripture tells us often run so counter to personal perspectives, that sooner or later the reader will come to a crossroads: either the Bible is completely out of date, or the Scriptures compel *us* to change *our* preconceived ideas and attitudes.

In the first place this applies to the universal call to repentance and conversion, to a return to God and submission to his authority over our lives. Here, the Bible demands a profound choice on the part of the reader, a choice that will influence all of life. Anyone who shrinks back from this surrender to the Creator will automatically keep the text at a greater distance. For such a person, the text itself comes across as untenable.

In the second place, the call to obey God is bound up with a broad range of conceptions that do not belong to the prevailing understandings of modern man, understandings moreover that cannot be scientifically verified. We think of the existence of heaven and angels, the aggressive enmity of God's great opponent, Satan, and the relationship between the visible and invisible worlds. In addition to these conceptions, the Bible also contains numerous events that cannot be explained through our scientific knowledge, such as a floating axe head, the drying up of the Red Sea, the immediate healing of the sick, and the raising of the dead.

It is impossible to separate a universal message in the Bible from the totality of these conceptions and events. It is good to face up to this from the start. There are many who believe that the stories of Creation and the Great Flood are to be understood symbolically. The same would be true of the various accounts of miraculous events. Even the virgin birth of Jesus appears to some as an untenable element of the enduring content of the Christian faith. But where does that end? After all, faith in Jesus' resurrection *necessarily* also implies faith in another, invisible world, and in powers that are beyond scientific explanation. And if Christ was not raised from the dead, then we are of all people most to be pitied (I Corinthians 15:17-19).

We cannot get away from it: the texts of the Bible presuppose the acceptance of a reality that is beyond our observation. Only those who accept this presupposed reality are able to read the Scriptures as credible and tenable texts. Those who are unwilling to accept this reality are compelled, in the end, to conclude that these texts themselves are totally untenable.

Does our reading of the Bible, then, require us to blindfold our understanding, or to sacrifice our intellect? That would be so if the books of the Bible claimed to be based on common human observation. However, the opposite is the case. The authors of the books of the Bible were only too conscious of the fact that they were writing about matters that are hidden from human eyes. They invite us to believe in the things hoped for, the things not seen (Hebrews 11:1).

We are unable to fit this unseen reality, and the powers that are part of it, into what we can see and scientifically investigate. This unseen world falls outside the capacity of human observation, even when equipped with the finest microscopes and the most powerful astronomical instruments. When the king of Aram besieged the town of Dothan, intending to arrest the prophet Elisha, the situation appeared to be hopeless. Even the prophet's servant cried out: *"Alas, my master, what shall we do?"* But then Elisha prayed that the Lord might open the servant's eyes, and suddenly he saw that *"the mountain was full of horses and chariots of fire all around Elisha"*. This other reality does not for a moment displace the observable reality of the surrounding hills: it does not take the place of our spatial existence. It does, however, exist simultaneously with it, be it invisible to the human eye (II Kings 6:15-18).

Those who wish to read the Bible may not close themselves off from God's unseen reality, a reality that transcends the for us observable creation. Whether the text of the Bible is still tenable for us depends in large part on our openness for the mysteries of God. Where such openness is lacking, and where we try to limit ourselves to what human eyes can see and human understanding can explain, the Bible will have lost its enduring meaning. In that case, the only question that remains is this: which has really become untenable, the Bible or (post)modern man?

Conclusion

Different times and a different world-view give us no cause to *a priori* characterize ancient texts in general as out-of-date and lacking in credibility. To do so would be to absolutize the view of reality of our own time as timeless truth, and to close oneself off to the lost wisdom of earlier generations. This is certainly no less true of the Bible: a book that owes its existence to the words of holy men, driven by the Spirit of God; a book that deals with seen *and* unseen realities.

CHAPTER 3

Bible and translation

Almost everyone reads the Bible in translation. Sometimes, certain translations have functioned as the authoritative standard: for example, the Latin Vulgate, the English King James Version or the Dutch *Statenvertaling*. Where that happens, readers are often scarcely aware of any difference between the ancient Biblical texts (Hebrew, Aramaic or Greek), and their rendering in another language (Latin, English or Dutch). However, once readers are given the opportunity to compare their own translation with another one, or have access to a number of widely varying translations, confidence in any particular translation will diminish. There are so many translations, but what does the Bible *really* say? Can we really rely on what we read in a translation of the Bible? And what criteria must a translation satisfy in order to be considered acceptable?

The answer to this question is complicated. In this chapter, we will discuss a number of aspects of the process of translation: the original language and the original text; words and sentences; passages and documents. At the conclusion of this chapter, we will consider the degree of confidence we can have when we read the Bible in translation.

Original languages
The Bible was first written in Hebrew (almost all of the Old Testament), Aramaic (particularly some parts of Daniel and Ezra) and Greek (the New Testament). The Scriptures have been handed down to us in these languages, and are usually translated from them. Sometimes we can tell for certain that the written text in the 'original language' is itself a rendering or a translation of what had earlier been said or written in another language.

For example, what God said in Genesis 1 preceded the emergence of the Hebrew language. The words spoken by people in Genesis 1-10 (the period before the Babylonian confusion of languages in Genesis 11) were in the one language (unknown to us) that was spoken by all people before that time. Paul's address to the Jewish crowd in Acts 22:1-21 was in Aramaic, and not in Greek. The tradition of the church holds that Matthew wrote his Gospel in Hebrew (Aramaic?), and that the original Greek Gospel that we possess is actually a good Greek translation of what he first wrote. Historically, that is interesting, but it has no significance for the exegesis of the text: what is decisive is the language in which the text was first written down and preserved for us. This is the language that we ought to uphold as the 'original language' for our exegesis.

Ancient languages

This does not mean, however, that in our study of the original languages of the Bible we should ignore related languages of their own time. For the study of the Hebrew text, knowledge of other Semitic languages is vital, since next to the Bible itself, there are virtually no other written texts that have been handed down to us in ancient Hebrew: the comparative material that we need to establish word meaning, or to understand their language forms, is almost totally lacking.

In addition, the Old Testament was written across a period of many centuries, and that is reflected in the wide range of language variations that we encounter. For the analysis of Biblical Hebrew, the use of analogous data from contemporary and related Semitic languages is therefore of great importance. All this data enriches our knowledge of Hebrew language, in which the Old Testament was written, and in this way it is of benefit to the translation and exegesis of the text.

The same applies to New Testament Greek. Here, the situation is much more favourable, because there is a wealth of comparative material available in Greek texts from various periods and a range of social strata. The authors of the New Testament usually came from social strata in which the use of two or three languages was commonplace, and the Greek they used shows evidence of that. In addition, these authors were often (consciously or unconsciously) influenced by the Greek of the Septuagint (the earliest Greek translation of the Hebrew Old Testament). Anyone who wishes to accurately interpret New Testament Greek not only needs to possess a sound knowledge of Greek itself, but must also understand the way other languages such as Aramaic and Latin might have influenced the Greek. Here too it is clear that all of these aspects, through an enriched knowledge of the original Greek text, indirectly benefit both the translation and the exegesis of the text.

Anyone who wishes to carry out a translation must be able to work independently with the original texts, but mastery of these languages is not given to everyone. In order to be able to come to an independent judgement, one must at the very least be so much at home in the *system* of these languages as to be able to independently read texts in the original language, and to evaluate commentaries on the basis of these texts. Whoever is not familiar with the *system* of these languages, and still wants to use interlinear translations to penetrate to the original languages behind the translations, will never get further than a kind of pseudo-knowledge. These interlinear translations offer a line-by-line and word-by-word transcription, to which is added a word-for-word 'translation'. It may appear that in this way the user of such an interlinear translation is enabled to compare the translation with the original language. This is largely an illusion, since the mere recognition of words is totally inadequate to make any judgements about the language and its translation: amateurishly consulting the original language often results in a distorted perspective (one that is exclusively focused on the comparison of words), and often does more harm than good.

The general rule is that the language of the original text ought also to be the source language for exegesis. Exceptions to this rule are sometimes made in the exegesis of the New Testament. There was a time when it was quite common to try to go back to a (conjectural) Aramaic source language for the exegesis of large parts of the Gospels.

From the perspective of textual history, such an approach is already quite questionable: it is by no means certain that Jesus usually spoke in Aramaic. The fact that some Aramaic words occur incidentally in the Gospels could just as well indicate that the use of an occasional Aramaic word stood out because at that time Jesus was speaking in Greek – as he often did.

From a linguistic-historical perspective, this approach is also not feasible: far too little is known about 1st-century Aramaic and its Judean and

Galilean variants, and other scholars argue that during this period Hebrew was still commonly used as the vernacular.

Exegetically, too, this procedure is quite dubious. Even if there had been an original Aramaic text, and even if this text might sometimes have had other possible meanings, then it is still the exegete's task to interpret the *language* used in the written *text* that has been handed down to us. After all, the writer of the Greek text, and its first readers, would also have had to understand the meaning of the text as it came to them in Greek.

We find an example of this in Matthew 3:9. In this passage, which deals with the preaching of John the Baptist, we read the following: "*...I tell you, God is able from these stones to raise up children for Abraham*". Various commentaries propose that this statement arises from the play on words between 'sons' (Aramaic: *'benayya:'*) and 'stones' (Aramaic: *'abnayya*). This play on words would only have existed in Aramaic, and would have been lost in the translation to Greek. The context, however, shows that John's *'these stones'* refers to the stones that lie scattered around him in the wilderness as he speaks (Matthew 3:4), and from Scripture as a whole it is evident that in Isaiah 51:1-2 a connection is made between the children of Abraham, and stones hewn from a rock: Abraham is the rock from whom Israel has been hewn. Against the background of this prophetic imagery, on which the Pharisees placed their reliance, John points out that God, who had once hewn children from Abraham, could just as well create offspring from *these* stones. God's *act* of creation is far more important than the material from which he forms them. Even if there had been a play on words in the Aramaic, it would have been no more than incidental, and it would not have provided the reason for this choice of words or expressions.

Treat language as language

The Bible tells us unique and unexpected things. It comes to us, not in the languages of angels, but of people. These are not new or technical languages, designed especially for this revelation: inspiration is not some kind of Esperanto. This implies that we ought to approach the language features of the Bible in the same way as those of any other text.

The process of determining word meanings should proceed in the usual way: the range of possible meanings of the word (as evident from the ways in which it is used in a variety of texts) is compared with its possible meanings within the specific context.

The scarcity of comparative material in non-Biblical Hebrew texts makes this process more difficult in Hebrew than in Greek, and that may well explain why this rule is not as consistently applied in Hebrew texts. As a result, Biblical Hebrew is sometimes regarded as a special 'language of revelation'; a view that sometimes extends to the Greek as well. As a result, greater significance is assigned to the etymology of words within the totality of language use than can be justified linguistically.

At the same time, disproportionate weight is given to concordant use of words. However, in many cases the *etymology* of a word (often referred to as its root meaning) is no longer semantically significant for the way it is actually used (*verba valent usu*: words derive their meaning from the way they are used).

In addition, concordance (equality) of word *forms* does not necessarily imply that the author also intended a concordance of *meaning*. Concordance of meaning can usually only be assumed if concordant forms occur within the same passage, and when the word that is used is not too common.

As an example, we may consider the Hebrew word *shalom* (peace). This word is derived from the root verb that means 'to be whole', or 'to be sound'. Even though any dictionary will show that this verb also conveys other meanings, the value of the word (or concept) *shalom* is then thought to derive from its etymology. The Biblical concept of 'peace' is then regarded as distinct from its present-day meaning in that it can no longer be defined as 'an absence of war', but rather as 'a state of complete harmony'. This view, however, disregards the fact that in the Bible the word *shalom* also has other meanings: sometimes it means no more than 'is he well?' (Genesis 29:6), or 'it's all right' (Genesis 43:23, NIV). Sometimes the word *shalom* actually points to a state of colonial subjection (as in Deuteronomy 20:10-12), a situation that modern theologians would not willingly qualify as *shalom*.

Similarly, the Greek *eiréné* (peace) has a much richer range of application than simply 'absence of war'. There was even a Hellenistic deity referred to as *Eiréné* (Irene). In English we might say: "Even after the peace treaty was signed, the situation on the ground was still far from peaceful". Of course, it is certainly true that the Bible offers the prospect of an all-encompassing peace: but this state could also be described without the use of the word *'shalom'* (as in Isaiah 11:1-10), and this revelation of Messianic peace forms no obstacle to other uses of the *words shalom* or *eiréné*. In Acts 12:20 (where the inhabitants of Tyre petition King Herod for 'peace') the word *eiréné* conveys a different meaning from that in Philippians 4:7 ('the peace of God which surpasses all understanding'). The deeper meaning of the word 'peace' in the latter text, however, cannot be inferred from the 'Biblical word' *eiréné* as such, but only from the juxtaposition 'peace *of God'* and from the context.

In both the Old and the New Testaments, there is a recurring danger in the application of so-called 'theological concepts', in that the dogmatic *concepts*, which are a distillation of Biblical revelation, are confused with Bible words themselves; these words are no more than elements of sentences, and in themselves do not form building blocks for 'concepts'. The Bible is not a lexicon!

An example of this is the Greek word *euangelion,* which could mean either 'the good news' or 'the bringing of good news'. The word could have this dual meaning because the *content* (the gospel) is unfolded in its *proclamation*. Actually, some have said, the good news only *becomes* truly Good News when the act of proclamation occurs. In this way, the 'gospel' becomes a relational concept, one that has no clear content apart from its proclamation. Linguistically however, this line of reasoning (and others like it) is rather odd. That becomes obvious as soon as it is applied to one's own language. In English, the word 'church' means 'gathering of believers' ("I belong to the church") as well as 'church building' ("tonight the new church is to be opened"). According to this reasoning, that would show that theologically we take the view that the church only becomes 'church' when it is in the building. This strange, quasi-theological reasoning overlooks the fact that we sometimes use the word 'church' metonymically, as in: '(the building in which) the church (meets)'. In I Corinthians 9:14 the word *euangelion* is used in its usual sense (the 'good news' that is 'preached') and as an abbreviation ('living from the gospel' meaning 'gaining one's living as preacher of the gospel'). It is even debatable whether it is correct to assign a second, independent meaning to the word *euangelion*: 'preaching of the gospel'. This kind of abbreviation (metonymy or other forms of brachyology) does not automatically lend legitimacy to the assignment of an equally valid second meaning. Consider the expression "he lives off the deacons": This use of language does not justify assigning an additional meaning to the word 'deacon': 'money collected by deacons'. In any case, the theological description of the relationship between the revealed message and the act of preaching cannot be inferred by identifying one possible application of the Greek word *euangelion* with another.

Original text

The Biblical texts have been handed down to us in ancient manuscripts that date from a time long before the invention of printing. The centuries-long process of successive copying (handwritten copies of copies of copies…) led to variations among these manuscripts, and consequently among the later, printed editions of the Bible. Before translators and exegetes can begin their work, they need to ask themselves what precisely the text is. This is a question that must, as a matter of principle, be addressed *before* translation or exegesis itself. Exegesis doesn't create text; it interprets it. And translators, too, must give first priority to establishing as closely as possible what the true original text is.

In order to make such a determination of the true text, the translator must be competent to make judgements about the history of the textual tradition. Such a judgement is not exegetical, but is to be based on historical research. Textual history is a separate branch of Biblical scholarship. Its outcomes benefit both translators and exegetes. As a rule, these scholars will strive to develop an independent grounding in the field of 'textual history'. Even if they do not become specialists in this field, they ought to be able to make their own informed judgements about the data that exists within the textual tradition. This prevents them from making choices among variants on the basis of inappropriate criteria (such as "this is easier to translate" or "this fits better with a preferred exegesis").

Once the text has been determined as accurately as possible, the translator and the exegete are bound to adhere to it. There may be problems in the chosen passage: these ought not to be taken away by smoothing over the translations, by changing the texts, or by transpositions in the text that are not justified by the history of the text itself. Difficult readings should then be provided with marginal notes, and exegetes are at liberty to propose suggested explanations for problematic readings.

In reality, this latter aspect also applies to those who insert more extensive changes within the whole of the text. This practice is often referred to as 'literary criticism', but in fact must be considered 'textual criticism'. By describing the process in these terms, it can also be more clearly shown how unfounded such techniques of contemporary exegesis actually are. We think of the exegetical approaches to a supposed 'Priests' Codex' (reconstructed from extracts *out of* the Bible books which had already been uniformly handed down as 'the books of Moses'), the interpretation of the Q-source (a reconstruction compiled from selections from the Gospels), or the commentaries on three letters to the Philippians (a reconstruction performed by breaking into separate pieces the present, uniformly handed down single letter to the Philippians).

One example of this practice concerns John 18:13-24. It is puzzling that the hearing before Annas (the high priest?, see vs 13 and 19) is discussed in detail, while no such detail is provided about the hearing before Caiaphas (vs 24, 28). In many commentaries, it is assumed that vs 19-23 actually describe the hearing before Caiaphas, and that v.24 originally came before v.14. These transpositions, and others like them, have been around for a long time (as early as the Syriac tradition), but cannot be justified on the basis of textual-historical evidence. Exegetes must then find their own answer to the question why the hearing before Annas is so extensively reported, and why he is referred to as the 'high priest' in this passage. One possible explanation takes into account that Annas, who had been deposed by the Romans, was still regarded by the Jewish community as the lawful high priest. John the evangelist shows, then, that the *de facto* (politically recognized) high priest aligns himself with the judgement of the rightful (ecclesiastically recognized) high priest.

Another example can be found in Isaiah 7:14. The earliest Greek translation (the Septuagint) of this verse reads: "…*you* (that is: son of David) will call him Immanuel". The child, born by way of virgin conception, is a child in the house of *David*. The Hebrew consonantal text (consisting of consonants only) supports this translation. The vocalized text (which has vowels inserted) reads: "…*she* will call him…". In this reading, the link to David is less obvious: it might appear that it concerns no more than a *woman* and her child. The specific vocalization of this text (in which the vowels are added to the consonantal text) is actually quite unexpected, and comparable to, for instance, Genesis 17:19. It presents an older Hebrew language usage, one that departs from the usage we find in Isaiah 7. Many commentaries still tend to accept this 'unconventional' usage. Since the interpretation of Isaiah 7:14 is hotly debated between Jewish and Christian readers, the possibility cannot be excluded that the (later) Jewish vocalization of this text was applied to somewhat weaken the connection between this child and the house of David, and so diminish its agreement with the account presented in Matthew 1:18-25. Taking this possibility into account, and in view of the differences between the earlier consonantal text and the unusual form of the later vocalization, there is scope to re-evaluate the authority of the reading of the Septuagint in this special case.

A third example is that of I Corinthians 6:20. Here, newer translations such as the ESV are shorter (*"...for you were bought with a price. So glorify God in your body..."*) than that of the King James Version: (*"For ye are bought with a price: therefore glorify God in your body, and in your spirit, which are God's"*).

In I Corinthians 6:13-19, Paul is discussing the body. For that reason, many exegetes consider the shorter version to be the correct one. However, the great majority of manuscripts have the longer reading! The omission of certain words or phrases in some manuscripts may be based on a similar exegetical logic, and that leads many contemporary scholars to have a preference for shorter (shortened?) texts. Quotations from the early church fathers are not of much use here, since their exegesis generally focused on the main thrust of the passage ('the body'); in such cases, there was every reason for a shortened quotation. It is clear, however, that Chrysostom had the longer text in front of him. The insertion of interpretive glosses was not a practice that occurred in the manuscripts; where then did the supposed insertion of *"which are God's"* come from? From the perspective of textual history, the case for the longer reading is very strong. Exegetically, this means that while Paul was chiefly concerned with the body (owing to widespread wrong practices at the time, arising from a *separation* of body and spirit), at the conclusion of his argument he did, however, arrive at a thetical statement affirming the *unity* of body and spirit (the foundational proposition for the manner in which Paul spoke about the body).

The scholarly practice of textual criticism does not resolve all problems. Sometimes the choice between two textual variants can be extremely difficult. In that case, it is better not to force a solution, but rather to present the alternative choice in the marginal notes (such as was done in the marginal notes of the Dutch *Statenvertaling*, and is still done in numerous English translations).

The exegesis that is brought to the congregation must, as much as possible, be based on elements of the text that are not open to debate, and that can be verified by means of the translation that is being used. The determination of the text must serve the exegesis, and ought not to get in the way of the congregation.

Readers of the Bible need not give up their confidence in the reliability of a Bible translation because there might be a marginal uncertainty in the determination of the original text, an uncertainty that might lead to different translations making different textual choices. As debatable as some of these specific choices might be, by far the greater part of the Scriptures has been unambiguously handed down to us. Uncertainty about a small number of phrases does not in any way give reason for uncertainty about the doctrine of the apostles and the prophets. On the contrary, this small margin of uncertainty can protect us against slavish adherence to the letter, and help us to fix our minds on the great promises and commandments that come to us in the Scriptures.

Words

Some readers of the Bible have a special fascination for 'Biblical words' and for the secrets they are supposed to contain. Since the Bible is now digitally accessible, the search for Biblical words has become very easy indeed. Very often, an electronic Bible is unlocked by means of 'search words'. Is this technological progress meaningful for the way in which we read the Bible? And how should we in fact come to grips with 'words'?

Words have meanings. And the meaning of a certain word (verbs, etc) consists of a combination of several *aspects of meaning*. Only rarely are all these aspects relevant to the way a word is used. The situation and context in which the word is used will lead the reader to understand which aspect of meaning is dominant, or which new aspect of meaning might begin to play a role in a new situation or context.

CHAPTER 3

Lexicons attempt to provide an overview of aspects of word meaning that might be applicable. As a rule, they do this by listing the various aspects of meaning that occur in general usage. Occasionally, this is also done by providing the words or phrases that stand in opposition: the meaning of a word is sometimes also determined by what it does *not* mean. Expressions such as 'a dry run' or 'dry wine' derive their meaning in part from the fact that 'dry' means 'not wet'. Lexicons are in essence the outcome of the reading of a multitude of texts and the observation of a broad variety of language usage. This implies that a lexicon ought not to be regarded as a list of meanings that already existed before the word came into use. Rather, lexicons are the by-products of a great number of exegeses: by hearing or reading and understanding words in their context the lexicographer arrived at a set of meanings for each word. Anyone who consults a lexicon as a tool for exegesis must understand that the lexicon does not precede the exegesis. While it may have less connection to the text than a commentary, it is not pre-exegetical.

A lexicon is an indispensable resource in the translation of a text. Its user, however, must always keep an eye out for the full range of meanings of the word. A quick search for the meaning the lexicographer had noted for a certain word in the passage is no more useful than consulting a translation or a commentary.

The distinctive value of a lexicon will only be used to its best advantage by examining the full breadth of possible word meanings: a translation or a commentary will not present this full range of meanings. They have made a choice. The lexicographer, too, made a choice, when he selected a citation as a source for one aspect of meaning. If we know what other aspects of meaning this word might display in this context, we could well conclude, in the totality of the exegesis, that the lexicographer was too quick in choosing for one and against another aspect of meaning. In the interplay between the (im)possibilities of word meaning and the (im)possibilities of context a way can be found to determine the actual meaning of the word in *this* text, and this is how the path to the translation is followed.

In the process of exegesis or translation, it is therefore important to consult as many different kinds of lexicons as one can lay one's hands on, while remaining aware of their varied characters. Some lexicons describe Old Testament Hebrew and New Testament Greek chiefly from within the bounds of the usage that occurs in Bible texts. The advantage of this kind of lexicon is that it often provides many instances of use in the Bible, and is able to go into much greater detail. On the other hand, the disadvantage of such a lexicon is that in them the influence of the compiler's exegesis is often greater than the user might realize. A second drawback is that the words are examined within an arbitrarily limited field. This effect is more pronounced in Greek than in Hebrew (see, however, the comment below). The authors of the New Testament used words that were current in their location and time. In order to gain a sound understanding of their language use, a general lexicon of the Greek language is highly desirable: the range of behaviours that fish display is better studied by scuba-diving in their natural environment than by observing them in an aquarium.

From time to time, independent study of word meanings may sometimes require the reader to work without the aid of a lexicon. A concordance (of Bible texts, but also of other contemporary extra-biblical material, such as Josephus or the Qumran texts) will then be a valuable resource to find the range of contexts in which the word occurs. Reading of literature from these contexts is an important aid to gain a 'feeling' for word meanings. The development of a sensitivity for language will also be greatly served by extensive reading of texts in the Bible (not just verses, but also longer passages, including extended passages from the Septuagint) and outside the Bible (such as Greek authors of the Hellenist period).

Those who are limited to their own language, and therefore to the use of a concordance in that language, will do well not to attach much significance to the fact that all the text references to any given word are ordered and listed together. These references often have very little in common, other than the word itself (and that often quite coincidentally). A concordance is actually not much more than a handy tool to find passages that not only share that one word, but are also comparable in other ways. The great drawback of concordances is that many comparable texts remain out of sight, because they (often by pure chance) do not contain the word one is looking for.

For example, in Psalm 31:20 David confesses about the Lord that *"...you store them in your shelter from the strife of tongues"*. The concordance tells us that the word *sukkah* is also used for the booth that reminds us of the Exodus. Do we read in this text an allusion to the Festival of Booths? A lexicon helps us to find the way. *Sukkah* means 'hut' or 'shelter', and it is used within this range of meanings. 'Booth' is one aspect of meaning that is especially relevant in the context of festive celebration. This festive context is not present in Psalm 31, and so it would not be correct to make a connection here to the festive booth of remembrance. Evidently, the word 'shelter' or 'hut' (and not the word 'fortress') has been chosen here to highlight that while the Lord will not keep David out of earshot of the strife of tongues, he will provide him with a place of shelter: this shelter owes its strength to the fact the Lord protects him here, and that is of more value than soundproof walls.

A second example can be found in Galatians 1:10: *"Am I now seeking the approval of man, or of God?"* The Greek verb *peithein* has two objects: God, and people. It seems as if Paul disapproves of winning the approval of people, and takes pride in seeking God's favour only. In II Corinthians 5:11, however, he speaks positively about 'winning' people – our translations commonly have 'persuade'): it is an office he has been called to. Examination of the manner in which the Greek verb form *'theon peithein'* (to persuade God) is used here reveals that it has an unfavourable connotation (to curry favour with God; to make God see things your way). This Greek usage helps us to better understand Galatians 1:10. Paul is not just out to win the favour of people. Rather, his aim is to persuade them, to turn people towards God, and not the other way around!

It would be wrong to always translate the Bible concordantly. The Scriptures are not interlinked with each other by a network of *words*, but by *thoughts* and *content*. The confidence of readers need not be diminished when words vary from one passage to another, or from one translation to another. What counts is that the message comes across faithfully.

Sentences

In the face of an excessive focus on (key) *words* in the Bible, we do well to realize that texts are not constructed in words, but in sentences (consequently, the usefulness of digital search programs is limited).

The sentence, not the word, is the basic unit of language use. In any given language, meaning is produced and understood within *sentences* by means of a complex system of rules. This system functions even when the user is unaware of it (such as in one's mother tongue). This system of rules, which we call *grammar*, gives us the ability to create meaning in sentences. And in any language (such as, for instance, Hebrew or Greek) it is the knowledge of its grammar that provides us with the ability to create and understand sentences that work within this system of rules. When using another language (whether speaking or listening, reading or writing), knowledge of its (unique) system of rules is required. The study of grammar assists in developing an awareness of these systems. It teaches us the meanings of variations in word forms, prefixes and suffixes, word order and syntax, etc. All these aspects of sentence structure contribute to sentence meaning. A sentence is not an empty container with words randomly inserted: within the sentence words are joined together in particular ways, rather like the pieces of a jigsaw puzzle. The actual aspects of meaning of individual words within the sentence are partly determined by the sentence grammar. That is why both translators and exegetes must always pay careful attention to the grammar of Bible languages.

For those who only have a limited knowledge of Bible languages, there are some aids to understanding, in which – verse by verse – the language forms are grammatically (and lexically) identified. Such 'crutches', however, will only be meaningful if they are used to find one's way (back) to an understanding of the grammatical system as a whole. There is not much point in collecting traffic signs unless one knows the road network to which they refer.

Anyone who is able to use the rules of grammar should keep in mind that this collection of 'rules' has come into being inductively, just as a lexicon has. The author of a grammar handbook has, in a certain sense, also had to make exegetical decisions in exploring the sentences of the text, and in determining the relative significance of text features he encounters. While it is true that a grammar handbook can achieve a high degree of objectivity, the prior assumptions of its author will sometimes influence his work. A grammar handbook, no matter how well-compiled, cannot be used as if it were a railway timetable!

It is also important to have an eye for the idiom of the Bible language, and also for the personal idiom of some of its authors. Modern grammar handbooks will have a better eye for this than older ones. Biblical Hebrew has all kinds of formal features that jump out at present-day readers, accustomed as they are to their own systems of grammar. This does not mean, however, that these features are just as striking or remarkable within the Hebrew language itself. Recently, a striking example of failure to recognize this was provided in a radio broadcast, when the speaker claimed that a characteristic feature of Hebrew language is that it proceeds from 'the other', while the starting point of Westerners was 'the self'. After all, it was claimed, Hebrew verbs are conjugated from the (simplest) 'third person' while in most Indo-Germanic languages verb conjugations begin with the (simplest) 'first person'.

The personal idiom of Bible authors can be most clearly understood when comparative analysis of word and language forms is undertaken and ordered separately for each individual author. Then it becomes apparent that the distinction between the Greek prepositions *apo* and *hupo* is not as clear-cut with Luke as it is with James. Some commentaries go to some lengths to point out that a specific word is positioned for emphasis in the sentence: in one instance, it emphatically comes first; in another, it just as emphatically comes last. This shows that in Greek the stress upon a specific word cannot always be determined simply by its position within the sentence. Having an eye for the personal idiom of individual authors teaches us to see whether a characteristic language form is semantically relevant, or whether its relevance exists on another level (for example, in indicating the idiomatic language use of a particular author). Everything in every sentence has a certain function, but not everything necessarily functions at the same level!

An example of this in Hebrew grammar can be found in Judges 17:6. The standard grammar of Biblical Hebrew teaches us that the normal word order in a sentence is: predicate – subject – object and/or adverbial phrase. It is precisely because of this rule that a departure in word order (such as in Judges 17:6) has a special function. "*Everyone – what was right in his own eyes – did*": here the emphasis is placed on the fact that everyone did what was right *in his own eyes*. The accent on this meaning in this sentence could only be ascertained through a study of grammar as it relates to word order in Hebrew sentences.

Another example, from Greek grammar, is provided by Mark 3:21. In the ESV this verse reads: *And when his family heard it, they went out to seize him, for they were saying, "He is out of his mind."* In the Greek, this is expressed quite strongly: "He has lost his mind". Is this the conclusion drawn by his family, his mothers and brothers (ch 3:31)? Scholars of grammar have pointed out that Mark often uses the third person plural to indicate the impersonal 'they', and does this without any clear change of subject (as in 5:14, 6:43, 6:54-55). In Mark's personal idiom, this verse can also be translated as "...for they said..." (that is: ...for *people* said ... as in the RSV of 1951). In other words, Jesus' relatives are spurred into action because *people* are starting to say that he is losing his mind. If his relatives had themselves really been of the opinion that Jesus had lost his mind, Mark is likely to have written the sentence differently: ...*kratèsai auton, legontes hoti exestè*. Exegetically, the interpretation that this refers to what *the public* said is supported by the fact that 3:22-30 talks about what people were saying, while in 3:31 Jesus' relatives send a message to Jesus, and obviously address him as being accountable for what he says and does.

An example of grammatical presupposition we find in John 9:3: "*It was not that this man* (the man born blind) *sinned, or his parents, but that the works of God might be displayed in him*". N. Turner wants to free this text from 'fatalism' by stating that *hina* ('so that...') does not have the usual purposive meaning (relating to a final outcome) here, but instead the *hina* is to be understood as an imperative. In other words, argues Turner, Jesus was really saying: this is not a matter of guilt at all. On the contrary, "Let the works of God be displayed in this man!" However, Turner overstates his case. Careful examination of the texts that are advanced in support of this imperative function of *hina* leads to the conclusion that of the 31 instances cited (in various grammatical texts), only 5 could truly be regarded as not referring to an end or *purpose* (Mark 5:23, 12:19, II Corinthians 8:7, Ephesians 5:33, Revelation 14:13). Moreover, in each of these cases the context provides additional indications that they refer to a desire or a command. That is not the case in John 9:3. After all, the disciples are not asking *to what purpose* the man was born blind, but the *cause* of his blindness. This cause is not to be found in his own sins, or the sins of his parents (v. 3a), but in the goal of his blindness. He had to be born blind, so that "...*the works of God might be displayed in him*". The preposition *alla* ('but') in v.3 points to a certain contrast (not this, but that), and also indicates that what follows in v.3b also needs to be linked to the question, why this man had to be born blind. Jesus' reference to the providence of God ought not to be massaged away by introducing a supposedly imperative *hina*. The fact that this providence does not leave room for any kind of fatalism is evident in the fact that Jesus *heals* the blind man.

Passages

The unit of language utterances is the sentence. Just as a sentence may consist of only one word, so a text may consist of only one sentence. That, however, is not the general rule. More often than not, a sentence consists of more than one word, ordered within a single sentence structure. In the same way, a text usually consists of more than one sentence, linked together within a single textual unit.

For the process of exegesis, it is important to know within which textual unit the words and sentences have been placed. When reading written texts of some length, we can readily distinguish smaller and greater exegetical units: the smallest units of meaning are in their turn included in a broader body of text.

When dealing with statements in Scripture, the broadest exegetical unit is the Bible as a whole. In actual practice, smaller units of meaning, such as a prophecy, a gospel or a letter are usually more significant. However, the most important unit of exegesis – certainly to begin with – is the smallest unit of meaning, one that cannot be further subdivided into discrete passages, segments or paragraphs. We call these units of meaning 'passages' or 'pericopes', and most Bible translations are subdivided into such passages, each with their own heading.

In *historical books* the smallest unit of exegesis is usually indicated in a narrative unit in which time, locations and persons are connected in a given account. Changes of location, action and/or time are usually indicated, and also contain a cue that a new event is to follow: a new narrative unit coincides with a new event.

When, in a historical book, a recount is given of a verbal address, this smallest unit can often be quite large. Instances of this are the discourses recorded in Matthew (such as in ch 10:5-42) and in Acts. In the account of an extended body of instruction, such as the Sermon on the Mount, smaller units of meaning within it are often indicated by thematic shifts or the use of a repeated refrain (Matthew 5:21, 27, 31, 33, 38, 43).

In the *prophetic books,* the smallest units are often indicated with introductory or concluding formulae, such as "*Thus says the Lord: …*" or "*… declares the Lord God of hosts*". Many prophetic books are in fact built up by a number of separate, but internally related, prophecies.

In an *epistle,* the unity of the whole is in principle much stronger. In practice, this is easily seen in shorter letters such a Philemon or II John. The longer letters, however, have not been written in one breath, and they display an internal structure of interconnected segments. Often these segments are marked by an *inclusio* (a closing statement that refers back to an earlier opening sentence), concluding remarks, or a clear change of subject. This interweaving of smaller units in a letter is generally far more intensive and more significant than the interconnection of smaller textual units in historical or prophetic books.

The practice of exegesis must begin by taking some distance from the chapter-and-verse divisions, punctuation, layout (paragraphing and spacing), etc. that is found in our own Bibles. In many cases, of course, the exegete will conclude that the suggested subdivision and formatting of the text is quite correct. However, he must come to this conclusion independently, making use of the structural features apparent in the text itself. Sometimes, the exegete will discover that the text requires a different structural ordering. The smallest textual unit is the minimum unit of exegesis: statements made within this unit of meaning should never be interpreted separately from an exegesis of the textual unit as a whole in which they occur. This will prevent literalistic errors and sermons built upon catch-phrases. Something that is common courtesy in dealing with human texts (do not interrupt the speaker) must certainly apply when we read the Bible. Unfortunately, owing to the frequency of our Bible use, this rule is only too often disregarded.

A characteristic of this incorrect approach is that sentences in the Bible are often regarded as 'texts', while in fact the sentences ('verses') are actually smaller elements of a larger textual unit. Just because we see numbered sentences in the Bible, does not yet mean that these sentences are 'texts'. After all, the network of chapter and verse divisions has been overlaid upon the Bible at a much later date! Chapter and verse divisions are a handy tool for finding one's way in the Bible, but they also have a great drawback: they suggest a textual 'atomism' that is quite out of place. It is therefore preferable that translations of the Bible incorporate very small and unobtrusive chapter and verse numbering, in order to ensure that the unity of the passage is clearly discernible, and to invite the reader to read the whole of the passage as the author intended.

An example of this is found in Rahab's 'white lie' in Joshua 2:4-6. The untruth she told about the departure of the spies from Jericho has often been a subject of discussion. The exegesis of Rahab's 'white lie' – including the moral judgement that accompanies our perspective on what she said – may not overlook or disregard the smallest unit of exegesis in which it is embedded: Joshua 2:1-24. This implies that her 'white lie' is to be interpreted – in part – using the background information she herself supplies, in ch 2:9-13. Here, it is clear that Rahab was not afraid of Jericho's rulers, nor of the spies. On the other hand, she understood only too well that the people of the God of Israel would soon put her and all of her compatriots to death. In this mortal peril she defends herself, and tries to save her own life by helping the spies. Anyone who raises an ethical question here must consider whether an entirely justified fear for one's life allows an act of self-defence, including an untruth. Attention for the passage in which this act is recorded lifts the moral question to a higher level than just a 'white lie'.

Another example can be drawn from Isaiah 53:1. Here we read:

> *"Who has believed what he has heard from us?*
> *And to whom has the arm of the Lord been revealed?"*

Is this verse an expression of astonishment about the incredible acts of God, or is it a complaint that no-one believes these great works? The manner in which this verse is quoted in John 12:38 and Romans 10:16 clearly assumes the latter. Now Isaiah 52:13-53:12 must be regarded as a textual unit: in it the Lord speaks of 'my Servant'. Whatever he says about this Servant is briefly summarized in ch 52:13-15. He shall be exalted after many were astonished at him. Many nations and kings shall see what they had not been told, and understand what they had not heard. And now in ch 53:1-12 this is worked out in more detail. Here, it is their failure to recognize the Servant that is highlighted (vs 1-10). After that, his exaltation and the salvation of many is briefly restated (vs 11,12). Since ch 53:1 clearly resonates – and contrasts – with ch 52:12, and where it also introduces the broader description of the failure of God's people to recognize his Servant, ch 53:1 is to be read within this exegetical unit as a complaint that Israel will respond with unbelief to the coming Servant of the Lord.

A third example can be found in Romans 1:27. Here, Paul writes that *"men gave up natural relations with women and were consumed with passion for one another, … receiving in themselves the due penalty for their error"*. What is the connection here between sin and punishment? The words of ch 1:27 constitute one element of the smallest unit of exegesis, namely ch 1:18-32. The error that is exposed here is that people imagined themselves to be gods, and failed to honour their Creator (ch 1:21-23). What follows in vs 24-32 is a consequence of *this* general error (compare the reprise in v. 28). God so radically abandons to their own desires people who place themselves above God, that in the end they no longer wish to experience anything more than their own image, which is actually the image of an idol. In their homosexual dissipation (Paul is talking here about heterosexuals who in indulge in homosexual practices!) the character of God's judgement upon a humanity that has surrendered itself to itself is revealed in its greatest clarity. Not because this kind of debauchery is the only one that deserves condemnation, but because it demonstrates most clearly and openly the nature of God's punishment upon their lawlessness: he lets mankind destroy itself.

This passage as a whole, the smallest exegetical unit, casts a clear light on each of the elements within it. Bible reading, focused on complete textual units, must begin with passages, and not with words or sentences.

Documents

Literary context

The passage or pericope is the essential stepping-stone within the totality of the text. In the end, what we are concerned with is the apostles' and prophets' writings as a whole. They did not hand down words, sentences or passages, but books, letters and gospels. Each and every passage must be read and understood within the context of the whole document. This is its literary context, and this context will provide us with an awareness of the distinct focus, the core intent (the 'scope', see ch 2, p.62) of the text.

CHAPTER 3

In Chapter 2 we already discussed the manner in which this concept of 'scope' has sometimes been abused. No-one, having established the core intent of a passage, may dismiss any of its elements, simply because they might not directly proceed from its scope. However, it is also true that neglecting the scope of a passage is just as harmful for a balanced and appropriate exegesis.

A number of indicators can be listed when considering the intent of a passage. And the *literary context* is the most significant of these indicators. In the first place, this relates to the intent of the literary whole (a book, a letter) and in the second place to the intent of the section in which the passage is located. The latter is the most specific and relevant, but it cannot be considered in isolation from the former.

A few remarks about both: the focus or intent of a literary text (an epistle, a book) is sometimes explicitly stated (Proverbs 1:1-9; John 20:20-31; Revelation 1:1). More often, however, it becomes apparent in the structure of the whole (the *toledoth* structure of Genesis; the progression Jerusalem-Judea-Samaria-Rome in Acts), or in the tendency that is implicit in the text as a whole (the Law-based evaluation of history in the books of the Kings; an exhortation not to fall away in Hebrews). With the exegesis of the smallest unit of a literary whole, the direction and intent of the whole must continually be kept in mind.

At the same time, one must be prepared to concede that this *overall* intent may sometimes have less relevance to the exegesis of the passage being examined. Often, it is the intent of the *section* in which the specific passage is located that will have a more direct bearing on its exegesis. Sometimes there is a formal demarcation of these sections (a group of prophecies about surrounding nations; a chapter containing a number of parables), sometimes the various elements are implicitly linked (Isaiah 7-12; I Corinthians 12-14), sometimes it is its focus on a similar situation (the stories about Elijah; the 'travelogues' in Luke). In the exegesis of texts that directly address an audience (prophecies, sermons, letters), their focus on an existing situation will be highly significant for the exegesis of the whole.

By way of example, we could compare I John 4:8 (*"God is love"*) with Hebrews 12:29 (*"our God is a consuming fire"*). Viewed in isolation from their historical and literary contexts, these statements could be regarded as contradictory. They are located, however, in different historical contexts: Mount Sinai (Hebrews 12:18-21) and Golgotha (I John 4:9-10) respectively. The literary context of I John points to the apostle's persistent efforts to persuade his readers that faith cannot go hand-in-hand with a lack of brotherly love (I John 2:9-11; 4:7-8). The statement "God is love" is not intended to furnish a comprehensive description of the nature of God; rather, it is aimed at people who want to serve God without showing any love. That would be impossible, for God himself *is* love! The literary context indicates that John wants to exhort his readers to listen carefully to God.

In Hebrews, the writer's statement is not intended to provide a comprehensive description of who God is, either. The literary context shows that the readers are reminded that in the New Covenant they have been called to a greater glory. Let us give timely attention to what we do, for just as formerly Mount Sinai trembled, God will once more "*shake not only the earth but also the heavens*". (Hebrews 12:26-27) God will then be a consuming fire for those who rejected Christ, or slackened in his service.

We find another example in the healing of the demoniac in the region of the Decapolis. Mark and Luke tell the story of only one demoniac (Mark 5:1-20; Luke 8:26-39); Matthew mentions two (Matthew 8:28-32). A careful comparison of the passages shows that it was not both that were possessed by a legion of demons, but just one of them. It appears that this legion-possessed demoniac had a companion with him. While Mark and Luke focus their attention on just the main character, Matthew highlights the total number of those that were healed. In Mark and Luke, the focus on the *one* man arises from their intention to tell how he becomes a preacher of the Gospel in the Decapolis. The structure of their accounts demonstrates that: the story concludes with his preaching. What was Matthew's motive for mentioning *both* of these men? This is clear from the literary context of Matthew 8-9. After the Sermon on the Mount, Matthew presents all kinds of evidence of Jesus' power and authority. That is why Matthew's attention does not focus on the outcome (the gospel is preached in the Decapolis); rather, he directs all his attention to the extent of the healing, and the deep impression that this made on those who witnessed it.

As an example from the Old Testament, we can point to the list of Milcah's children in Genesis 22:20-24. The positioning of this list in the text intentionally draws attention to the contrast with Abraham, who left Haran, and who in the end received just *one* son; a son, moreover, whose life was preserved only through a substitutionary sacrifice (Genesis 21:1-22:19).

Style

The intent of the author is also evident in the *style* of his presentation or narrative. The same account, or the same thoughts, can be expressed in a number of different ways. The style the author chooses to use is not irrelevant to his intentions: the style of narration or formulation provides means to accentuate, intensify, emotionally charge, or lend appeal to what is written. Anyone who in his exegesis neglects the author's style will lose something that belongs to the text. Since in the process of translation some elements of the author's style can easily be lost, an exegete ought to return to this aspect separately once the previous stages of translation have been completed.

Style (the author's individual manner of speaking) is distinguished from *language form*. *Language forms* are conventional: they are common to users of a specific language, place and time, and the author of the text uses these commonly accepted forms to represent facts and thoughts. On the other hand, authors are free in their choice of *style*: even though they are limited to expressing their thoughts within the framework of given language forms, they are not bound to conventional patterns in giving voice to their style, their individual expression as an author. Adjectives and adjectival forms are resources available to them, and the author is free to use them or not. The totality of an author's language choices, the inclusion or omission of certain words, the use of a broad range of language structures and/or word combinations constitutes the author's style. Since these aspects are the results of the author's choices and the free composition of text, they are properly considered to be an object of textual exegesis.

In some contemporary theories of translation, the idea that the same thing may be expressed in a number of different ways is too dominant. Pragmatically this view might be quite correct. Exegetically, however, it is not so simple, since the exegete is dealing, not only with the *content* of the matter (a narrative, a thought) but just as much with the *manner* in which the author articulates this content. Transforming the text by restructuring it might not by definition be harmful to the realities it conveys, but it will be detrimental to the textual presentation of those realities. It is clear enough that Biblically faithful dogmatics can never replace the text of the Bible itself. However, it must be equally clear that a translation of the Bible that focuses exclusively on 'meaning', and not on modes of style and expression, also does an injustice to the authors of the text. It is therefore to be applauded that a number of contemporary Bible translations (such as the English NIV and ESV, and the Dutch NBV) have devoted a great deal of attention to the style and the language register of the text. Style may sometimes have little influence on the informational aspects of the text, but it will always have a great influence on the level of emotion, beauty, positioning, etc.

Of course, it is not so that style, the manner in which thoughts are expressed, exists completely independently of conventional practices and usage patterns. We could say that style always involves a balance between the use of common language forms and the expression of the individual. An excess of the former will result in texts that are full of clichés and quite devoid of interest. An excess of the latter will lead to texts that are so individual as to become unreadable, or at least incomprehensible.

This composite nature of style implies that a grammar text, while it may have some useful things to say about style, is still very limited in this regard. The exegete will still need to carefully consider the degree to which the author's style does (or does not) conform to prevailing stylistic forms of his own time.

Conforming to existing language styles is common, and occurs for a variety of reasons.

The pattern of complementary parallel sentences or clauses (also referred to as *parallellismus membrorum*) frequently occurs in Old Testament poetic and prophetic literature. This poetic form is also found outside the Bible. It assists in memorization, creates poetic effects, and can also (such as in the Proverbs) be used to establish or highlight a specific point. Exegesis must take this poetic form into account. The relationship between two parallel sentences (as in Old Testament poetry) must be interpreted differently from, for example, two successive sentences in a line of argument (such as in one of the New Testament letters).

Prophetic literature often presents the stylistic form known as the 'Botenspruch'. By means of an introductory or concluding "Thus says…"

a direct statement of the Lord is very precisely delineated, and the reader is also alerted to the fact that this is a direct statement intended as a literal message from God to his people. The function of this (what to us may seem rather repetitive) "thus says…" is determined by the author's style.

In those parts of the Bible that have a legislative intent, a certain casuistic-legal form is quite common. This form of expression also occurs outside the Bible. In this form, rules of justice are made concrete through the use of specific examples. The example provided points in a general direction, and serves to teach a certain attitude. Having an eye for this stylistic form keeps us from reading these casuistic stipulations in a legalistic manner, or in a way that limits their reach.

In the world of Hellenism, the form of the *diatribe* was widely used: this was a fictional discussion with an imaginary opponent, and served to draw attention to an important point. We come across this form in parts of Paul's letters and in James. This is a lively approach, and it involves the reader personally in the argument. We can be certain that Paul and James selected this form of address intentionally and thoughtfully: they were not just used as some kind of cliché.

The Semitic world was sensitive to the beauty of repetition. Lists and repetitive passages that Western readers might find monotonous were intended as a stylistic device to highlight the serious or festive character of a text; readers ought also to place themselves in the setting of texts being read aloud to a largely illiterate audience. The repeated account of the building of the tabernacle (first the design, and then its execution) and the lists recorded in Numbers are illustrations of this form. While we would be inclined to condense the text of Numbers 7 to one-twelfth of its actual length, the exegete must learn from this stylistic form the notion that the Lord regarded the gifts presented to him as highly festive and solemn, and must make an effort to track down the reasons for that.

In both the Old and the New Testaments, we come across narrative forms where the event is first summarized briefly and then the account is recounted in detail from the beginning. For a listening audience, this was a suitable tool to keep track of the story line. Exegetes must recognize this stylistic form in order to avoid misunderstanding. The commonly held view that the five wise and five foolish maidens lay quietly sleeping somewhere along the roadside in the dead of (a chilly) night is the result of misunderstanding the stylistic form of the narrative. After all, Matthew 25:1 tells us what this story is actually about: young women who bring their lamps and go out to meet the bridegroom. In ch 25:2-5 the preliminaries are first described (five of them neglect their preparations). It is not till v.6ff that the story about the lamps going out and the maidens attending to them actually begins. In other words, the maidens were asleep in the banquet hall. And the advice of the others to quickly go and buy some more oil from the merchant is more realistic when it takes place in the banquet hall (in the village) than at some distant place out in the country (ch 25:9).

To round off this section on the recognition of existing stylistic forms, there is a need to warn against the inaccurate use of the concept of 'form'. In many theological works, 'prophecy', 'apocalypse', 'wisdom literature', or 'healing narratives' are regarded as stylistic forms, existing genres of literary expression, in which the use of this particular form does not claim to convey real predictions concerning the future, genuinely received revelations, true wisdom, or accounts of actual healings.

However, these kinds of texts are not stylistic devices, or ways of expression; rather, they are authentic expressions of how things actually are. Of course, it is always possible to inauthentically employ a fictional text form (invented or false prophecy; nonsense presented as wisdom literature; telling a story about recovery from illness to convey hope for the future). But the fact that it could be possible to use such text forms in a fictional manner only exists because these text forms are not used as versatile weapons for verbal combat, but as existing tools with an established claim to authority. The narrative form of *Max Havelaar* (a 19th century Dutch novel, written to expose the evils and abuses of the colonial system in the East Indies – tr.) is what gives it such a serious tone: while it is a work of fiction, it aims to be taken seriously as something that conveys true history. The author of a book about World War II does not select the narrative form as one of a number of equally valid options, but because this war really happened, and therefore requires presentation as a "historical narrative". The stylistic forms and devices the historian might choose in writing the work is another matter. Within the genre "historical narrative" the historian is free to choose from a wide variety of styles. We may not try to camouflage the fact that it is the Lord who speaks in a prophecy by representing these text genres as stylistic forms that human authors might have selected as just another expressive tool.

Individual expression is most clearly recognized in a text by asking oneself a number of questions: why has the author written the text like *this*? Couldn't he have used other means of expression to discuss the same matter; would he have chosen *this* style of expression intentionally? In many cases, the author – if we could have asked him – might have replied that he hadn't really given it much thought. And that is why we need to take care not to impose forced explanations. Anyone who thinks that the author had intentionally chosen *this* formulation, and not some other, would have to be able to draw on other indications in the text, so that one piece of evidence is supported by another.

A related question that might be asked is this: why does the author record the historical account or point of doctrine like this, and not in some other way? Why does the author concentrate on one aspect of the event, and remain silent about another? Some elements in the parable of the ten minas (Luke 19) are not elaborated on: why not? Is it because Luke is asking attention for something else? Luke must have known how things turned out with Simon the sorcerer in Samaria (Acts 8). How does the fact that he concludes his account without mentioning the outcome function in the whole of his narrative? Genesis 12 tells us that Abram was showered with gifts when Sarah was brought into Pharaoh's court. The narrator refrains from making an explicit judgement about that, but doesn't the inclusion this piece of information function indirectly as strong criticism of Abram's behaviour (he profits from keeping silent)?

In cases where one text has a parallel in another, comparison of the two texts may be useful to uncover its distinctive features. I Chronicles 21 identifies Satan as the instigator of David's decision to count his fighting men. II Samuel 24, however, points to God's anger burning against Israel as the cause. The New Testament gospels offer numerous examples of stylistic differences in the accounts of the same events. Attention for these differences sharpens the readers' awareness for the meaning of the text.

Translation and clarity

Often, translations will not (fully) live up to the reader's expectations. Readers of the Bible generally expect a translation to be quite clear. And yet, reading the Bible, including in translation, often proves to be quite challenging. Expecting translators to provide an easy-to-read translation of the Bible in all its parts is therefore too much to ask. It just doesn't work that way. And that is so for several reasons:

1. The Bible is composed of a variety of texts that differ considerably in level and clarity

2. The texts of the Bible presuppose a great deal of background knowledge about their setting, and that knowledge is not always readily available to the present-day reader.

3. The Bible demands a strong faith involvement from the reader, and that involvement is sometimes lacking.

Translations may not attempt to compensate for these obstacles. A successful translation uses the receiving language (such as English or Dutch) clearly and responsibly, and it does not make the translated text easier or more difficult to understand than the original. A better and more complete approach is to provide marginal notes, which indicate the degree of certainty (or uncertainty) of its translation choices. It may also insert information that is implicit in the text. In the absence of such marginal notes, readers are left to their own devices.

The problem of the relative (lack of) clarity of the Bible is not always due to the translation. At times, you can hear people say: "But it's only a translation". Implied in this statement is the suggestion that knowledge of the original languages would dispel any uncertainty. This notion, however, is incorrect. Knowledge of the original languages will, of course, assist in evaluating the translation on points of detail, but it is no help in fully clarifying everything. Readers of a translation are therefore not at a principle disadvantage, and they are not disempowered by the experts. It is precisely because of translations that one is able to read the Scriptures *in their totality*. That also helps us to be quite certain about what *is* clear in the Bible.

While the Bible (and Bible translations) will never be totally clear, the clarity of the Bible's revelation about God, Jesus Christ and the Holy Spirit is quite compelling. Unresolved questions about translation details need not stand in the way of reading the Bible with confidence. This is also partly due to the fact that there is a great deal of redundancy in the Bible, so that we are never dependent on just one word or just one sentence. This abundance in revelation, and the fact that the Word has become flesh gives us confidence in our Bible reading: *"Long ago, at many times and in many ways, God spoke to our fathers by the prophets, but in these last days he has spoken to us by his Son"* (Hebrews 1:1,2).

CHAPTER 4
Bible and history

Biblical texts come to us from a distant past, and they have their origin in different historical periods. A unique feature of the Bible is that it consists of different parts that came into existence over a period of about 1500 years, and that almost two thousand years after its completion it is still being read. Reading the Bible without taking this history into account would degrade a collection of historic documents into a timeless codex.

Two historic threads run through the Bible, and each of them demands our attention. In the first place, there is the line from the past to the reader: the time of origin in history of each separate text (the times of the texts). In the second place, there is the connecting history of all of these documents (the history of revelation).

At the same time, there is also the line of history from our own time back to that of the text: what role does contemporary history play when we read this book that comes to us from the past, and exists within the whole of a coherent history of salvation?

The texts and their time
In the Bible we encounter texts that have been written in languages other than our own. Hence, they have to be brought to us in *our* languages by means of a process of translation. These same texts also come to us from the past. And it is especially in translation that this becomes very clear: they haven't been written in our own time! That compels us to travel back in our imagination to the time of the text. In order to properly understand a language product, we need to have a good understanding not

only of the language, but also of its time. Texts are linked, in all kinds of ways, to the time in which they came to be. These links are almost always implicitly assumed.

The situational framework of any language utterance contributes to its intended meaning. And the less those who have come later know about that framework, the harder the text will be to understand. That is why texts from times past increasingly need explanation and clarification, so that later readers are brought to the point where the original readers began. This information is not itself the interpretation of the whole of the text, but it is an indispensable part of it. Anyone who understands the time in which the text was written is favourably positioned to clearly and accurately receive the intended message of its author. It may be that such a message runs contrary to the time and author of the text, but we would only be able to discern that when we are able to compare the text with its time. Here we intentionally do not say 'the time of the *author*' or the time of the '*message*', but 'the time of the *text*'. Authors may far transcend their own time, and it would not be proper to *a priori* limit the author's horizon to that of their time. In the case of the Bible, that is self-evident: the Lord, the Inspirer of the Bible, does speak *at* a certain time, but he is not bound *to* that time. Whoever understands the texts of Bible at a text-archaeological level (that is its language and time) still only stands at the foot of Mount Sinai. Still, that is where we must begin: that is why we pay attention to the time of the text.

We come to grips with the situational framework of the text on a number of levels, the most common of which we will briefly touch on here. Each of these levels requires its own resources, and it is only Bible encyclopaedias and Bible dictionaries that provide information at all levels. The drawback of these quick guides, however, is that they provide little information about their internal connections. It is therefore advisable, in addition to a good Bible encyclopaedia, to also obtain a number of monographic overviews for various specific subjects.

Topography and geography

Bible texts provide accounts of many historical events that take place in regions and locations that are assumed by their authors to be well-known. For later readers, then, a good atlas is indispensable. Often, a proper understanding of the text is hardly possible if one doesn't know where the events that are described take place. The reader should also be alert for changes in topography across the passage of time.

For example, Ezra 4:9 refers to the judges and officials of the "*province beyond the River*". This is not (as in earlier books of the Old Testament) 'the region beyond (to the east of) the Jordan'. The centre of government in Ezra's days was located in Persia. From that perspective, 'the River' was the Euphrates, and it was the region to the *west* of the Euphrates that was known as 'the province beyond the River', in other words Syria, Palestine, etc.

We find another example in Luke 24:50. There we read that Jesus led his disciples out of Jerusalem "*as far as Bethany*" (in Greek: *heoos pros*). The Ascension took place on the Mount of Olives, and that is hardly in the vicinity of Bethany. Luke's choice of words is puzzling: what does 'as far as' mean? A study of the layout of roads at the time shows that, on leaving Jerusalem and traversing the Mount of Olives, the traveller would come to a fork in the road; at this point a side-road left the main road and led to Bethany. It is worth considering whether this might not clarify the expression in Luke 24:50: they walked on till they came to the 'turn-off to Bethany'. The Ascension turned this two-way junction into a surprising three-way!

Flora and fauna

There are no camels in Papua New Guinea, and the olive tree is not native to Holland. The Bible texts are written among rock badgers and myrtle trees. Anyone who wants to understand the Bible of Jacob's day must together with Esau breathe in the odour of the open field. A good resource book about the flora and fauna of Palestine will be more of a help than a tourist trip to Palestine. The authors of the Bible not only *saw* plants and animals; they were closely familiar with them. Their texts bear witness to that.

An example: in I Kings 21:19, we read that in the place where the dogs licked up Naboth's blood, they would also lick up the blood of Ahab and Jezebel. We need to realize that these are not the same kind of dogs that today's Bible readers would pay a dog licence for. These dogs were wild scavengers.

Another example is found in Matthew 13:24-30: the parable of the weeds among the wheat. The Greek word *zizanion* is much more specific than our 'weeds' would lead us to believe. It refers to darnel or ryegrass (*Lolium temulentum*). At first, it is indistinguishable from wheat; only when the ear develops (and the roots become entangled) can it be recognized for what it is. This aspect is not unimportant when we consider whether this parable could be applied to illustrate the 'advantage' of a 'people's church'.

Political history

Rulers of Philistine towns, Pharaohs in Egypt, a proconsul in Corinth and a city clerk in Ephesus all leave their traces in the Bible. The exegete must therefore search out the various kings and Caesars of bygone ages. A good handbook that deals with the history of the places and times in which the Bible texts are located is therefore indispensable, along with an historical atlas.

For example, Isaiah 7 presupposes that its readers will know that at that time Assyria was a regional threat, against which the coastlands of the west endeavoured to unite. Aram and the kingdom of the ten tribes made a treaty. Judah, shielded by these two territories, chose to remain neutral, and so keep its options open. The attack by Aram and Israel upon this potential threat from the rear (Judah) provides the background to Isaiah 7. The prophet's reference to Assyria (v.17ff) becomes clearer to those who are familiar with the political map of the period, even though the root cause lies in God's plans to punish his people (at the hands of the Assyrians).

Acts 12:1 describes '*Herod the king's*' actions against the church. But which king Herod is meant here? Luke assumes that his readers will be able to tell the various Herods apart. This Herod is a different one from Herod the Great in Luke 1:5 or Herod Antipas in Luke 13:31. While Herod (Antipas) in Luke 23:7 has no authority in Jerusalem, Herod (Agrippa) in Acts 12, does. Here, the Bible assumes an amount of background knowledge that we, by means of a catch-up course, first need to make our own.

Culture

Culture paints its own picture, and it has its own history that may not always run parallel with political history, even though the two undoubtedly influence each other. By the 'culture' of the time of the text, we mean customs, morals, prevailing practices, laws, social situations, etc. Overviews of the customs of any Biblical period are often extensive (and expensive). In many cases, one may have to be satisfied with a selection of monographs, which together provide enough information about the culture of the time. Books about 'Bible times' may provide some information about social situations, but usually offer too little about laws and morals. That is quite understandable, since morals and laws are often subject to significant change, and may vary greatly from place to place.

Genesis 16:4-6 may serve as an example here. This passage tells us how Sarai humiliated Hagar, after Abram, hearing about Hagar's arrogant behaviour, had said: "*She is your slave; do to her as you please*". Sarai raises this conflict with Abram as a legal matter: "*May the Lord judge between you and me!*" (v.5). In the light of the *Codex Hammurabi* (a Babylonian legal code, engraved in stone, and dating to an earlier period than Abram), this is quite understandable. This Codex shows (lines 144-147) that in those days rules of law applied to situations where a slave woman who had been promoted to concubine started to behave with unseemly pride: such a concubine could not be sold, but she could be demoted back to being a slave woman (compare Genesis 16:3: "*Sarah … gave her to Abram her husband as a* wife" with 16:6: "*she is your* slave". Abram puts Hagar back in her place in response to his wife Sarai's lawful demand). The angel's instruction in ch 16:9: "*Return to your mistress and submit to her*" is in the first place an instruction to Hagar to return to the place to which she, *according to established law* of the time, had been assigned. Of course, knowledge about this period does not yet mean that here the last word has been said about Abram and Sarai's actions: they were called to be *more* than 'children of their time'.

A second example can be found in I Corinthians 7:21. Here, the apostle Paul encourages slaves, and writes about slaves who have the opportunity to gain freedom. Should the latter take advantage of this opportunity, or should they remain slaves? Exegetically, opinions differ at this point. Close study of the social position of slaves in this period of the Roman empire reveals that a slave could be either freed or kept as slave by the decision of his or her *master*: slaves themselves were not given a choice in the matter. The text, therefore, should be interpreted in a different direction: a slave who was given freedom (thanks to the master's decision) was called to use this freedom well. This is not a matter of choosing – or not choosing – to act upon an opportunity, but to make the best use of a given situation.

Religions

The Lord's revelation enters a world full of superstition and idolatry, confronts it, and is opposed by it. A sound knowledge of the religions of the time is essential to be able to make sense of the shouts of the worshippers of Artemis in Ephesus, or the clamorous wails of the priests of Baal at Mount Carmel. The message of many religious ordinances in Israel had to do with their radically different starting points, compared to those of the surrounding nations. Books about 'Bible times' often provide information about other religions of the period. Next to them, the use of monographs is to be recommended: they usually do not have the distorted portrayal that so often arises from the one-sided perspective of books-about-the-Bible, which focus only on those matters that the Bible touches (or seems to touch) on.

For example, the temple of the Lord is a closed temple. There is no image in it. Temples were found throughout the whole ancient world. Pagan temples always contained images, and were partly or wholly open to the public. This contrast places a strong emphasis on the *closed* condition of the temple, rather than on the fact that Israel *had* a temple. This closed character has a significance of its own: it highlights the holiness of the Lord and the uncleanness of the sinner; in so doing it raises the expectation of the coming Mediator, who is to unlock free access to God (Hebrews).

Another example: in I Thessalonians 2:1-12 the apostle seems to commend himself with a great deal of self-satisfaction. In this whole passage, however, Paul draws a clear contrast between himself and the swarm of travelling peddlers of religion from the East, who were spreading throughout the empire. They depended on making a big impression, on an intimidating presence, and on extracting large sums of money. Paul, on the other hand, presented himself in a quite different way. He was less clever (without 'flattering speech'), less authoritarian, less impressive. He was second-best when it came to making an impression. But he acted as he did because he gave precedence to the Word of the true God, and not the words of men (ch 2:13).

The history of revelation

In the previous section we discussed the 'time of the text', the world in which the text was written down. In order to understand the text, knowledge of this world is essential: the text presupposes such knowledge. However, as regards its content, the text itself can stand well outside its time and its world. The time in which the text is written is by no means always the most significant context for its message. The attack on the World Trade Centre on September 11, 2001 will be hard to make sense of for anyone who does not understand the world of the late 20th century. And yet the *historical context* of this attack is to be sought in the various streams of thought within centuries-old Islamic religion. It is no wonder that after the events of September 11 there was a sharp rise in the sale of books dealing with the history of Islam and various streams of fundamentalism within it.

The historical context for the texts of the Bible is to be found in the history of God's revelation. Prophets and apostles built upon the Word that had been given long before. At the centre of this history of revelation stands the Lord Jesus Christ. In order to understand the texts of the Bible we must become acquainted with the progress of the history of salvation, and with the various stages and climactic moments it contains.

The carrying off into captivity of the kingdom of the ten tribes can be dated during the period of the Assyrian empire (the time of the text). However, this captivity is not to be described as simply one part of the history of the Assyrian empire. It has its own historical context: the history of God's promises to Abraham, the law given to Israel, the temple of Solomon, and the worship of the golden calves at Bethel. This historical context is extensively worked out in II Kings 17:7-23. The historical context is not always described as explicitly as that. However, it is always presupposed. An expression such as '*and it remains to this day*' should be interpreted with reference to the first readers and is intended to make a connection between the (older) narrative and reality as these readers experienced it. The refrain we hear in Judges: "*In those days there was no king in Israel*" clearly alludes to a later time, in which there *was* a king in Israel. The Old Testament often harks back to the experience of the Exodus from Egypt. Similarly, the New Testament repeatedly draws on the experience of Gentiles who, by the power of the Holy Spirit, had come to faith (see Galatians 3:2-5; Hebrews 6:4-5).

As we read the Bible, we must always place its various documents in the light of the previously described facts of revelation. In Acts 16:3 we read about

Timothy's circumcision *"because of the Jews"*. This circumcision stands in the historical context of an earlier decision by the apostles, declaring that Gentile Christians were no longer required to be circumcised (Acts 15:28; 16:4). From the context it is clear what value Timothy's circumcision does *not* have. It could not have been anything more than an action taken for the sake of the Jews, who otherwise might have thought that Timothy was unwilling to be circumcised for the sake of his earthly father (a Gentile). It is for the sake of the *heavenly* Father that the uncircumcised had to be accepted in Christ without needing to be circumcised.

We can and may use extrabiblical sources when investigating the *time of the text*. However, our study of the 'history of *revelation'* must draw on the Bible, and the Bible alone, as its source. From the Bible we deduce a summarizing and coherent history of Gods revelation through the centuries.

The question could be asked whether we, in this way, do not arrive back at 'contextual reading'. In principle, of course, it is true that taking the historical context into account is one of the ways in which we 'compare Scripture with Scripture' (in other words, contextual reading). Still, we must distinguish here between contextual reading within *one* book or epistle, and taking account of the historical context in its entirety. From a literary perspective, the book of Genesis does not provide a context to the prophecy of Nahum. The unity of Scripture does not, in itself, require that the historical context operates at the same level everywhere. The unity of revelation does, however, mean that the historical events of revelation *as a whole* form the historical context for each of its constituent parts. The historical account of Genesis *is*, in principle, part of the historical context for the book of Nahum.

The history of revelation recounts the succession of special events that Scripture makes known to us: beginning with Creation, through the calling of the patriarchs, up to the sending out of the apostles in the power of the Spirit of Jesus Christ. This long history, recorded in the Bible (sometimes in broad outlines, and at other times in detail), forms the stage setting: against this background the texts speak! Attention for this history of salvation serves to sharpen the focus and renders the details more easily discernible.

a. *Persons* may already, at the moment of the text, have a historical significance, or fill a meaningful role. Owing to the fact that it is the reformer-king David who commits adultery with Bathsheba, this sin takes on a special, negative meaning (cf. II Samuel 12,14a).

b. *Places* can sometimes be closely linked to the recollection of past events. Samaria, in the New Testament, cannot be separated from the Old Testament history of the kingdom of the ten tribes (see John 4:5,20). In Hosea 2:14, the Valley of Achor that becomes a door of hope is not just any valley: it is the historic valley that lay close to Jericho (the people of God must start from the beginning, but it has to be a *fresh* start!)

c. *Action*s may have a symbolic meaning; they may also recall a previous event. The laying on of hands has a spiritual significance: recognition and blessing. When Jesus 'touches' a leper (Matthew 8:3), in cleansing the leper from his uncleanness, he symbolically takes the leper's uncleanness upon himself.

d. *Times* may be connected to earlier times. Events that take place at certain feasts are sometimes linked to the commemorative value of the feasts themselves.

e. *Images* may have added value, specifically in their references to earlier history of revelation, or to similar images of the world at that time. In the former case, we think of the imagery used by the prophets, calling to mind the wilderness journey, or other events, or the New Testament imagery that points back to the Old Testament (the lamb, the vine, etc). In the latter case, the animal symbolism brings to mind the symbolism of the imagery used by Assyrian and Babylonian kings. As to the jasper and carnelian (in Revelation 4:3) that describe the likeness of him who sat on the throne: during that period, rulers ornamented their robes with precious stones, since at that time gemstones served more as symbols of male authority than as ornamentation for females.

f. *Quotations* from earlier texts often evoke more than just the explicit reference. In Bible times, the audience often knew their Scripture by means of regular recitations, which could then be recalled by the simple reference to key words or sentences. Together with the memory aid itself, the whole text or passage it referred to was recalled. One can compare the 'brief' quotation (from Isaiah 40:3) in

Matthew 3:3 with the more 'extended' quotation in Luke 3:4-6 (Isaiah 40:3-5). This is a different effect from what is evoked in Bible readers like ourselves, who largely know their Scripture through reading it for themselves, and who are accustomed to the use of chapter-and-verse references. Quotations such as those in Matthew 2:15 and 2:18 can only be fully understood when one keeps in mind the context-evoking effect of such quotations. An example of such references to whole passages can be found in James 2:5ff. Here James (implicitly) brings to mind the Sermon on the Mount, where the kingdom of heaven is promised to the poor (Luke 6:20): when in the same breath, James refers to the motif of the rich, who for the sake of the Name persecute Christian believers (ch:6-7), this runs parallel to what follows in the Sermon on the Mount. The same is true for ch 2:8-10, where James speaks against the background of Christ's instruction about 'being perfect' (Matthew 5:47). In a similar fashion, Micah 5:1,2 provides a summary of the elements we find in Isaiah 7-12.

The time of the reader

The Bible is a collection of texts from earlier times, and in these Scriptures we read about the special history of God's dealings with this world. We ourselves live in another time, and today's readers of the Bible often do not experience the same strong connection with the history of God, starting in Paradise. The perspective of the reader can sometimes be quite different from the perspective of the text itself. Today's reader, as an involved participant, may sometimes be tempted to expect too much from the text, and to lift it out of its context. When considering the topic 'Bible and reader', we ought not to look in just one direction: that of the Bible's historical context. We must also look in the other direction: our own historical context as readers.

Frequently readers of a later period come to an older Bible with all kinds of questions drawn from their own personal or social situation, in search of specific texts that can provide definitive answers to their questions. Or we pick up the Bible in order to find in it confirmation of our own convictions or customs, which have arisen at a much later time in the church or in a Christianised culture.

There is a significant danger that questions of our own time or church situation begin to exert an influence on our readings of the text. There is a real risk that the readers insert themselves into the text, and impose their own convictions or questions upon it. Just as a lock can be forced by using the wrong key, a text can be forced by imposing on it a question that does not fit.

Sound exegesis looks in two directions. There will always be a difference in level between the text and the reader's situation. It would be wrong, as many modern scholars do, to speak of a chasm that can only be crossed by a (hermeneutical) 'leap'. Even as a general proposition, it is untrue that 'yesterday's' texts have no relevance for 'today'. And it is certainly untrue in relation to the Bible (see chapter 2). However, this connection must only be made with careful consideration. In a canal, the waters on both sides of a lock are connected to each other: a navigable channel exists between the two sides, in both directions. One must take time, however, when negotiating the lock's gates, to deal with the differences in water level on either side. In the same way, there must be a transition between the exegesis of a text and its application in the present. Readers must have knowledge, not only of the text, but also of themselves. This will prevent them from being only able or willing, like Narcissus, to see their own reflection mirrored in the surface of the water.

After all, readers often come to the Bible because they are busy with other questions and want answers to them. These 'other questions' may arise in a variety of fields: dogmatics, politics or aspects of everyday life, to mention just a few. For example: while engaging in a discussion about homosexuality, one might suddenly embark on an exegesis of Romans 1, sometimes with a hidden agenda: perhaps to neutralize the text, or possibly to harness it in support of one's own point of view.

Similarly, those who oppose changes in the liturgy of worship may focus on texts that appear to have something to say about New Testament liturgy, after which these texts will then be used to set boundaries within which liturgy ought to be confined (this happens in churches, which in adhering to the Regulative Principle of Worship, interpret the Bible in a restrictive sense).

Or a scholar of dogmatics, wishing to articulate the doctrine of election, will immerse himself in the exegesis of Romans 9 or Ephesians 1.

There is something positive to be said about such situations: after all, wisdom is sought in the Scriptures. At the same time, there is a hidden danger in such activity: consciously or unconsciously, one's own preferences (or perhaps even prejudices) are brought in. On the basis of these preferences certain texts are highlighted, while other parts of Scripture may be overlooked, or texts divorced from their contexts, making them say more than, or something different from what was originally intended.

Most often, this desire for a conclusive exegesis arises in the following areas:

1. Formulation of confessions and dogma (in which proof texts are sought in support of confessional and dogmatic statements, or to refute exegeses or texts advanced by heretics);
2. Ethics (in which ethical commands and or recommendations are based on specific Bible texts);
3. Church polity (to legitimize the offices, provide guidelines for church government and congregational development, and establish rules for church discipline);
4. Catechesis (to provide examples for instruction);
5. Liturgics (Biblical information for liturgy and songs).

This desire can arise incidentally in various areas, inside as well as outside of theology. On an individual basis, people may be led in their choices for future directions or the upbringing of children by texts that they come across and seem to be decisive in reaching a particular conclusion.

In all these cases of Bible application, careful attention should be given to whether questions arising from one's own problems or interests are being forced upon the text that this text was never meant to answer, or whether later history has not imperceptibly come to overlay an earlier one. All too often, in the course of history, there has been a tendency to approach the text – in a manner of speaking – as a pickpocket, to extract from it something that the questioner has no right to. Our Saviour's instruction about truthfulness in our speech (we may not have two kinds of truth, one under oath and one without it) was not directed at later questions raised by Anabaptists (given the permanent obligation to speak the truth, might there be situations where an oath is required due to reasons apart from the speaker?). The question whether cousins might be allowed to marry cannot justifiably be asked of Leviticus 18: this passage addresses all kinds of unchaste behaviours 'within the family'. In surrounding nations some behaviours were accepted or tolerated within the family that outside of the family would be considered shameless. The law of the Lord shows that the same rule applied within as much as outside the family! This issue is a different one from the question addressing which degree of kinship relations may or may not be permitted when engaging in a lawful marriage. There may be points of analogy, but we must also take into account the differences between the situation of the text and our own situation. In a case like this, the application should be externally confirmed, which here really is not the case.

In order to avoid unjustified applications of Bible texts, the following course is recommended:

1. When reading the Bible, make time for critical self-examination. Knowledge of the Bible and knowledge of oneself need each other. It is wise to explore, not only the historical context of Bible texts, but also the background of our own modern problems or questions. It is especially by taking the historical differences between the text and later questions into account that the way can be opened to the enduring wisdom of the Bible and its constant ability to give direction in other times and places. The Bible is a compass; it is not there just to be copied!

2. It is preferable to avoid working with concordances. All too often a modern concept or topic is used as a starting point to find a concordant word or expression in the Bible, and the places where such a term occurs are then gathered together, while neglecting or ignoring historical contexts or limitations. For example, when considering whether blood transfusions are allowable, all the texts containing the word 'blood' are brought together; when considering the task of elders, all the places, without distinction, where the word 'elder' occurs are listed, etc. Instead, one should always exegete each text, as a whole, within the textual unit where it occurs. Only then is it possible to address the question whether this text provides connections (either directly or by analogy) with a sought-for application or a given problem. Besides, it often happens that texts that do not contain the specific word or concept may well have much

to say about the topic in question. For example, there are texts that tell us much about the wrath of God, in which the word 'wrath' itself does not occur. The Bible as a whole may have more to say about an ethical problem within the whole of our attitude to life, than we realize when we are searching for a quickly and easily applicable word in a concrete situation. The Bible's compass teaches us to look further than the fork in the road that is right before our noses!

Conclusion

In order to read the Bible with confidence, it is important to know not only the time in which the various texts were written, but also and especially the all-encompassing span of time of God's coherent deeds: within the framework of this *one* history the texts arising from various periods of human history will gain their own colour, and we will discern all of them as belonging to the same Lord.

All of this will also help us not to approach our reading of the Bible all too readily from our own time and experience. While the Bible is not a manual providing instant answers to problems that arose later, it is a reliable compass to find a navigable path in other times, and to keep a steady course.

CHAPTER 5
Prophecy and fulfilment – the prophetic word

The Bible can be characterized as 'the prophetic Word' (II Peter 1:19). The holy Scriptures were either written by prophets themselves, or present a record of what they preached (Genesis 20:7). Moses was the greatest of Israel's prophets (Deuteronomy 18:15,18; 34:10). Samuel was attested as a prophet (I Samuel 3:20); David, the poet of the Psalms, was also called a prophet (Acts 2:30). Right up to the time of the kings of Israel, it was the prophets who played the chief roles in the recording of the Scriptures. It is well known that also during the era of the kings themselves, the prophets recorded and evaluated the events that took place. The Old Testament ends with prophets who cry out from captivity, or who bear witness to the restoration of Jerusalem. At the end of the Old Testament period, we meet the great prophet, John the Baptist. Jesus, who came after him, is even more than a prophet. He is the very Son of God. The apostles that he sends out are, as the envoys of the Son of God, in a comparable position to the prophets of the Old Testament: the apostles, too, speak with the authority of the One who sent them (Galatians 1:6-9). And the New Testament concludes with the prophecy of the Book of Revelation (Revelation 22:10, 18-19).

The Jewish historian Josephus observes that the defining characteristic of Jewish religious literature is that it was written by prophets; hence, it consists of only a small number of mutually harmonious writings, and not a large number of divergent books, as was the case with surrounding pagan nations. Since the prophets owed their knowledge of earliest history to the inspiration of God, and moreover wrote reliably about their own times, Israel possesses the most precious writings that are to be found in this world.[36] Tertullian, a Christian from the 2nd century AD, points to the excellency of the Scriptures: *"Whatever is taking place, was foretold,"* and *"Whilst we experience them we read of them, whilst we are examining them they are proved… Hence, therefore, we have also a sure confidence in future events, regarding them as in fact already proved, because they were predicted at the same time with those which are being verified daily. The same voices pronounce them, the same writings note them, the same Spirit impels them."*[37]

The prophetic character of the Bible also determines its reach. Prophets gain their knowledge from God. The Lord takes them into his confidence about the future. And by their mouths he speaks about things that do not yet exist. Abraham, the friend of God, hears what God's plans are for Sodom (Genesis 18:17). And the prophet Amos says: *"For the Lord God does nothing without revealing his secret to his servants the prophets"* (ch 3:7). Agabus, the New Testament prophet, is able to predict that a severe famine is to take place during the reign of emperor Claudius (Acts 11:28). Whether a word is truly prophetic may even be tested. God provides Israel with this criterion to distinguish true from false prophecy: *"When a prophet speaks in the name of the Lord, if the word does not come to pass or come true, that is a word that the Lord has not spoken; the prophet has spoken it presumptuously. You need not be afraid of him"* (Deuteronomy 18:22). The foretelling of events serves an important purpose in the revelation of God's counsel. The Lord speaks to his people through Isaiah as follows: *"Because I know that you are obstinate, and your neck is an iron sinew and your forehead brass, I declared them to you from of old, before they came to pass I announced them to you, lest you should say, 'My idol did them, my carved image and my metal image commanded them.' You have heard; now see all this; and will you not declare it? From this time forth I announce to you new things, hidden things that you have not known"* (Isaiah 48:4-6). This prophetic word has a broad reach; so broad that the prophet himself might not have grasped its full meaning. The prophets indeed saw the future, but often not all the way to its horizon. They *"searched and enquired carefully … what person or time the Spirit of Christ in them was indicating when he predicted the sufferings of Christ and the subsequent glories. It was revealed to them that they were serving not themselves…",* but those to whom the Good News would be preached (I Peter 1:10-12).

The phenomenon of predicting the future is not limited to the Bible. But the Bible is the only book that may, in its entirety, be called a 'prophetic Word'. After all, those words that speak about the future are not just incidental 'predictions'. They are organically joined to the whole of Scripture, and they form a unity with its description of the past and the present.

Future prophecy

Not all of the prophets' words are directed to the future. Parts of them deal only with the present, or with events within the lifetime of the prophet himself. Other parts, however, look forward to a future time.

Statements that relate to the future await a fulfilment. They are still to demonstrate their truth. Such words anticipate the events they refer to.

The time interval between future prophecy and the event predicted may often vary. Sometimes, the fulfilment takes place soon afterwards. In Acts 21:11, the prophet Agabus, speaking to Paul in Caesarea, foretells that he will be bound by the Jews in Jerusalem, in order to be handed over to the Gentiles. It was only a matter of weeks before this prophecy was fulfilled. Sometimes, the time interval between a prophecy and its fulfilment is much greater. Isaiah prophesied of a time when *"the leopard shall lie down with the young goat"* (ch 11:6), and we know that at least 28 centuries have elapsed between this word and its still-to-be-expected fulfilment. Such variations in interval may even be found within a single prophecy. At Shiloh, the prophet Ahijah was given a number of messages for the wife of King Jeroboam, when she came to inquire of him about her mortally ill child. His word that the child would die before she returned home (I Kings 14:12), was fulfilled almost immediately (ch 14:17-18). His prophecy about the destruction of Jeroboam's house (ch 14:7-11) was not fulfilled till years later (ch 15:29-30). And the fulfilment of prophecy about the deportation of Israel into exile (ch 14:15-16) did not take place until more than two centuries had passed (II Kings 17:5-23).

The content of the prophetic message will reveal whether it is a prediction for the near future, or whether it looks forward to a more distant time. David, the prophet, foresaw by the Holy Spirit the reality of a righteous ruler of the nations, who is to *"... dawn on them like the morning light, like the sun shining forth on a cloudless morning, like rain that makes grass to sprout from the earth*" (II Samuel 23:3-4). Comparing this foreseen reality with his own rule, and the rule of his near descendants, David realizes that this prophecy speaks of a future reality, for he immediately continues: "*…my house is not so with God!*" (23:5, NKJV). The family chronicle in II Samuel that precedes these words shows that all too painfully. In these verses, then, David is looking ahead to a much later time of fulfilment: "*For will he not cause to prosper all my health, and all my desire?*" (ch 23:5). David's last words look ahead into the distant future.

While future prophecy teaches readers to endure in their expectation, it is not suited to calculate later times or events. After all that he sees about future events, Daniel wonders in bewilderment what this will all lead to (Daniel 12:8). The only answer he receives is that "*… these words are shut up and sealed until the time of the end. Many shall purify themselves and make themselves white and be refined, but the wicked shall act wickedly. And none of the wicked shall understand, but those who are wise shall understand*" (ch 12:9-10). And when the Lord Jesus himself has spoken at length to his disciples about the last times and the final judgement, he concludes his instruction with: "*…but concerning that day or that hour, no one knows, not even the angels in heaven, nor the Son, but only the Father. Be on guard, keep awake, for you do not know when the time will come*" (Mark 13:32-33). The book of Revelation also, which is so full of prophecy about "*the things that must soon take place*", concludes with an appeal to the readers to sanctify themselves and to endure in their hope for the future (Revelation 22:10-20).

While future prophecy has not been given to enable us to map out times to come, it has been written so that we will recognize its fulfilment when it does come.

Fulfilment

Central to any future prophecy is its relationship to the coming of Christ. In the Gospels and in the apostles' discourses in the Book of Acts we find numerous statements about the way in which future prophecy is to be fulfilled.

Our Saviour often quotes from the (Old Testament) Scriptures, for these Scriptures show that he is the promised Redeemer. He fills in the blanks in the maps drawn by the prophets. He is the fulfilment of the Scriptures. And that is precisely his programme: he has come to fulfil the law and the prophets (Matthew 5:17-18). Let the Jews, by all means, keep on intently searching the Scriptures, *"… for it is they that bear witness about me"* (John 5:39). As Jesus reads the prophecy of Isaiah 61 in the synagogue at Nazareth, he declares that *"today this scripture has been fulfilled in your hearing"* (Luke 4:18-21). And when Jesus, at the moment of his arrest in the garden of Gethsemane, calms his disciples, he says: *"… but how then should the Scriptures be fulfilled, that it must be so?"* (Matthew 26:54).

The entire New Testament is founded on the conviction that future prophecies made in the Old Testament are still being fulfilled, and on the certainty that Jesus has come to fulfil them now and in the time to come. The apologists of the 2nd century AD did nothing more than to explain clearly to both Jews and Gentiles that their Saviour answered, in the most remarkable way, all the predictions for the future, predictions that predated by centuries those of the philosopher Plato, predictions that were read aloud every Sabbath day in the Jewish synagogue.

During that same century, the heretic Marcion launched an attack on the heart of the Christian faith when he began to teach that the Old Testament was the book of the Jewish god, the Creator, while the New Testament was a new revelation coming from the eternal Father. By separating the New Testament so drastically from the Old, Marcion actually severed the jugular vein of the Christian faith. Could he not see that in the letters of Paul, so beloved by him, there were numerous references and allusions to the Old Testament? Well, yes he did, but the point was that Marcion distorted the fulfilment of the Old Testament into an after-the-fact Christological interpretation. Now that the Sun of truth has risen, said Marcion, even the dead surface of the Old Testament moon has begun to shine; it is however a borrowed glow, a mere reflection. It is no prophecy-in-advance, already given by the Holy Spirit in the Old Covenant but an *ex post facto* reinterpretation by the Spirit of the New Covenant.

It is no wonder that the 2nd-century Christian church fought with all its might against Marcion and his teaching. It is, however, remarkable that in our own time Marcion's ideas have almost become commonplace in the Christian world. It is an almost universal assumption of modern, scripture-critical scholarship that the evangelists, influenced by their experiences concerning Jesus, arrived at a novel reinterpretation of the Old Testament. The thought that the Old Testament had already portrayed all of this beforehand is often dismissed with the scornful remark that 'prophecy' is something else than 'foretelling the future'. Of course, such a remark is a half-truth: 'prophecy' is indeed something entirely different from a fortune-teller's isolated and incidental 'predictions'. On the other hand, this remark is also totally untrue. Within the organic whole of prophecy we definitely do encounter predictions concerning the future. We intentionally use the word 'predictions' here, in order to show as clearly as possible that these are statements made at a much earlier time about events that are to take place later, and that in the meantime they have (in large part) actually occurred.

Since this is a crucial aspect of New Testament exegesis, we now return to the manner in which Jesus – and his disciples – spoke about the fulfilment of Old Testament prophecy. They did not merely *state* that prophecies were being fulfilled: the *content* of these prophecies also served as arguments in their teaching.

When the disciples must learn that Jesus *must* suffer and die, he begins to 'show' them (in Greek: *deiknuein*). What we have here is proof from the Scriptures: this is also why Matthew says that Jesus began to *show* them that the Christ must suffer (Matthew 16:21). After his resurrection, the Lord comes back to this activity of argument and demonstration, when he says: *"These are my words that I spoke to you while I was still with you, that everything written about me in the Law of Moses and the Prophets and the Psalms must be fulfilled"* (Luke 24:44). It is because of this instruction that the evangelists are later able to insert into their account the originally disbelieved teaching about fulfilment (see, for example, John 2:22). Matthew especially points to numerous prophecies in the Old Testament that Jesus fulfilled.

The manner in which the apostles conducted their debates with unbelieving Jews also shows that they really were arguing from the *originally intended meaning* of the Old Testament texts, and not from later interpretations or added meanings. Right up to his arrival in Rome, Paul consistently tried "... *to convince them* (the Jews) *about Jesus both from the Law of Moses and from the Prophets"* (Acts 28:23). What Paul was doing was presenting proofs from Scripture that Jesus is the Christ. From an exegetical perspective, these are straightforward proofs drawn directly from the evident meaning of the texts. The fact that these proofs did not always lead to faith is owing to the hardness of heart of his audience (Acts 28:25-27), and not to something out of the ordinary in the way in which these texts were read, understood or argued.

We find an example of this kind of argument from the text of the Old Testament in Peter's address on the day of Pentecost (Acts 2). He quotes from Psalm 16, where David is speaking of someone who will not be abandoned to Sheol, and whose body will not see corruption. Peter then places this word next to the facts: David died, and his tomb is still to be found in Jerusalem. Obviously, the Psalm is not referring to David himself. It must therefore be pointing to someone else. Who answers to this description? After the morning of Easter, Peter knows the answer: the Psalm points to Jesus, who was buried, but whose body was not abandoned to the grave. David was allowed to foresee in his time what was happening now (Acts 2:24-32)!

We find another example of such argumentation in Hebrews 4. The author reads Psalm 95 with his audience. There, we find a solemn warning: *"Do not harden your hearts"*. This warning comes with a threat. If you do, the same thing will happen to you as happened to the Israelites in the wilderness: they could not enter God's rest. Now, the author of Hebrews argues as follows: if the people of Israel had entered God's rest when they crossed over into the land of Canaan, then God would not have been able, later, to repeat that threat: *"you will not enter my rest"*. Clearly, then, the 'rest' God spoke about must have been something other than life in Canaan. This rest was somewhere else. *Repos allieurs!* Even for New Testament believers the rest is still to come: these warnings are meant for our ears too! In Hebrews 4, the use of a quotation from the Old Testament is based on an exegesis of texts in their context, not on forced interpretations of a selection of likely-sounding catch-phrases.

The hermeneutical rule for the interpretation of texts that point to the fulfilment of earlier prophecies assumes that these earlier texts (quotations from the Old Testament) are to be read and taken seriously as predictions concerning the future. The reader must also keep in mind that such quotes often drew on memory aids: there were as yet no chapter-and-verse divisions, and knowledge of the Bible was linked to its content. A whole Bible passage was often brought to mind by reciting a well-remembered phrase. This recitation of the phrase would then awaken in the audience's memory the whole passage in its context, even if that was not explicitly stated. Matthew 3:3 provides a good example of this. In order to ensure that his readers have a proper understanding of the work of John the Baptist, the evangelist refers to Isaiah 40:3. If the reference was limited to this one verse, then the thought could easily arise that Matthew's focus was on the word 'wilderness' (the place where John preached and baptized). Matthew's intention, however, is to point to what Isaiah already foretold: the promised proclamation of the coming of the *Lord* as Redeemer. This comes out more clearly in Luke 3:4-6, where in a comparable situation he also quotes from Isaiah 40, not only v.3, but also vs 4-5. Still, while Matthew has a shorter reference, he also has the whole passage of Isaiah 40:1-11 in mind.

Stages of fulfilment

Some future prophecies relate to a one-time event: these are fulfilled once only. An example of such a prophecy is Isaiah's foretelling of Hezekiah's recovery from illness, and the extension by fifteen years of his reign (Isaiah 38:4-8). The same applies to prophecies that unambiguously speak of a single event in the distant future. An example is the angels' message at Christ's ascension, that Jesus will return in the same way as he ascended into heaven (Acts 1:11). On the other hand, when future prophecy relates to a number of connected events, its fulfilment might involve various stages.

The book of Ezra begins with a joyful statement that the Lord stirred up the spirit of King Cyrus of Persia, so that in the very first year of his reign he proclaimed an edict throughout his kingdom, in which the Jews were instructed to rebuild the temple of the Lord in Jerusalem. This happened so that *"the word of the Lord by the mouth of the prophet Jeremiah might be fulfilled"* (Ezra 1:1). Jeremiah had sent to the exiles in Babylon a copy of the prophecy concerning all the destruction that was to come upon Babylon; they had to read this letter aloud, then tie a stone to it and throw it into the River Euphrates (Jeremiah 51:59-64). What was foretold about Babylon's destruction had been fulfilled. Implied in this prophecy, however, was also the message that the Jewish exiles would be allowed to return to Jerusalem. Cyrus' edict served to help make this prophecy come true. Still, that does not mean that the message of Jeremiah 50 and 51 has been exhausted. For we also read that there will be a return from exile to the regions of Carmel, Bashan, Ephraim and Gilead (Jeremiah 50:19); this return did not take place during the reign of Cyrus, but much later, in the period not long before the birth of Christ, when Jews again began to settle in Galilee and Perea. Moreover, it would be hard to argue that Jeremiah's prophecy relates exclusively to the geographic spread of the Jewish people. For immediately following those promises we also read: *"In those days and in that time, declares the Lord, iniquity shall be sought in Israel, and there shall be none, and sin in Judah, and none shall be found, for I will pardon those whom I leave as a remnant"* (Jeremiah 50:20). We find various elements interwoven in Jeremiah 50-51, because they form an organic unity (the destruction of Babylon, the return to Jerusalem, the restoration of the people, the forgiveness of sins). The realization of these things in the course of time, however, runs through a number of stages. The one follows the other. In hindsight, we can discern times and occasions, and determine the time intervals between the various events, but in the prophecy itself, we view these events through a telescope, as it were. They are superimposed in our view, and it is difficult, if not impossible, to estimate how far apart they are.

This phenomenon is often referred to as the 'prophetic perspective'. This is a useful descriptive term, provided we keep in mind that we are dealing with a complex structure of fulfilment, prophecies that have multiple elements. We ought not to lose sight of that, even for a moment. Only when we are dealing with extended and complex future predictions would it be useful to consider whether we are being presented with a foreshortened perspective, and whether we need to take various stages of fulfilment into account, since not all elements of a complex prophecy reach their fulfilment at the same time.

However, the expression 'prophetic perspective' is sometimes used when it shouldn't be. This happens when we are dealing with a prophecy – or an element of a prophecy – that is *not* complex: a single prophetic word is then thought to have undergone various stages of fulfilment. Terminologically, that is problematic: a simple prophecy – as opposed to a complex one – either has reached fulfilment, or it has not. It may be that some time is needed to complete the fulfilment of a certain prophecy, but it is not possible for a simple prophecy to be fulfilled a number of times in succession. In order to accommodate this problem, it is sometimes supposed that we may think of an 'initial' and a 'later' fulfilment, or of an 'initial' and a 'richer' one. Words like 'poorer' and 'richer' however, do not fit with the verb 'fulfil'. After all, 'fulfilment' necessarily involves the complete realization of a prophecy. The realization of a *fact* might be 'poor' or 'rich', 'disappointing' or 'pleasing', but the realization of a prophecy as such can only be measured by the standard of whether its fulfilment has taken place or not. One might answer the question: 'has this prediction been realized?' by saying 'partly', but not 'provisionally'. To use the expressions 'provisional' or 'richer' imposes a concept of 'fulfilment' that approaches the 'interpretation model'. In that case, there is no way of testing whether the fulfilment has taken place. Could there possibly be a 'richer' fulfilment at a later date? Such an interpretation of 'fulfilment' would remove itself from the actual meaning of the text.

For example: when in Joseph's dream, the angel tells him that the birth of Jesus to the virgin Mary is the 'fulfilment' of Isaiah's prophecy: *"Behold, the virgin shall conceive and bear a son, and they shall call his name Immanuel"*, the angel could not mean anything other than that Isaiah's word had not yet been fulfilled before, but has now reached such fulfilment (Matthew 1:23). In Justin Martyr's *Dialogue with Trypho*, the Christian speaker does not tire of showing that the Jews – quite contrary to the text of Isaiah 7 – apply this prophecy to the birth of Hezekiah. This 2nd-century Christian will have none of this compromise of an 'earlier' and a 'later' fulfilment. The angel himself does not speak of a 'later' or 'richer' fulfilment; the text simply says: *"This took place to fulfil what was spoken by the prophet..."* In Isaiah 7, too, this puzzling word about a woman (there is no mention of any man) is an unfulfilled word, given as a sign to the house of David. It is a sign that throughout Isaiah 7-12 is consistently portrayed as a mystery for the future (8:8; 8:10; 9:1-6; 11:1-10). In Isaiah 9:5, the exclamation *"To us a son is given!"* is an echo of the prophecy about a child that is to be born to the virgin.

Literal fulfilment?

American Dispensationalists often accuse many Bible-believing Christians that they do not really believe in the fulfilment of prophecy. After all, haven't so many Christians spiritualized the words of the prophets, and in so doing diminished their fulfilment by applying them only to the establishment of the Christian church, as if the prophets had not foretold the restoration of the state of Israel? Most of Christianity – so goes the charge of the Dispensationalists – has been blinded to a large part of these prophecies, in that it claims to want to accept the whole Bible, but neglects to interpret it literally!

Here, we come up against a central problem: what is the 'literal' fulfilment of prophecies that speak about the future of Israel? Millennialists (those who expect the coming of a 'thousand-year kingdom') explicitly portray this, not as an 'Israel-problem', but as a 'hermeneutical problem'. After all, it also comes into play when we consider whether the warfare spoken of in the Book of Revelation is to be understood 'literally' or 'spiritually'.

The debate, however, about 'literal' or 'spiritual' interpretation of some prophecies suffers, already in its initial stages, from the terminology that is adopted. For this terminology does not adequately cover the positions that are taken. If we take 'literal' to mean that we do not in any way consider the possibility of figurative expression, then the future prophecies in the Old Testament will be complete nonsense. There wouldn't be a single expositor who doesn't in some way take account of the occurrence of imagery and figurative language within any prophecy. Conversely, no adherent of 'spiritual' exegesis would ever go so far as to 'spiritualize' the reality of a new heaven and a new earth. It would therefore not be correct to get caught up in a dilemma that has been forced upon us in this way. The expressions 'literal-spiritual' are of no value in arriving at clarity about exegetical questions that might exist here.

Numerous prophecies have a poetic structure. They display parallel clauses, use hyperbolic and aesthetic language, and at times include imagery that is explicitly identified as such. If 'reading literally' means that we take the text seriously as it comes to us, then that means we ought also to take into account the style of the prophecy, and the implications arising from that. When the Lord says to Isaiah that he will *'make the heart of this people dull, and their ears heavy'* (ch 6:10), no-one will take that statement 'literally'. Why not? Because it is obvious from the context that this statement is using concrete imagery. When the Lord promises Israel that *"his shoots shall spread out; his beauty shall be like the olive, and his fragrance like Lebanon"* (Hosea 14:6), we are dealing not only with a comparison between Israel and the flowers of the Lebanon, but also with a non-literal description of Israel's future ('fragrance'; 'shoots spreading out'). Why is that immediately obvious? Because we have a great deal of prior knowledge about Israel, and about the way people 'grow'. In other words, as we read a 'literal' text, we take into account what we already know: this limits and directs the application of the text.

The same applies, however, to the reference to 'Israel'. Just as we cannot assume that 'shoots spreading' literally means 'the growth of shoots', we cannot automatically assume that 'Israel' is a direct reference to 'the Jewish people'. Here too, we must ask what we already know about Israel. What does the Lord reveal about this nation? To what extent does this prior knowledge determine the application of the prophecy, either to 'the Jewish people' or to 'the people of God, Jewish *and* Gentile'?

The 'literal' reading of Old Testament prophecies is in fact often not a matter of 'literal reading', but of reading with blinkers on. One reads the text, but does not look around to see what else is already known. This is not the place to for an extensive discussion of God's revelation concerning the place of Israel in his plan for the world. We do know, however, that the existence of the people of Israel is a means in the hand of God to ultimately extend, after a period of concentration upon one people, his blessing to all nations (Genesis 12:1-3). From the cradle of its existence, Israel exists for the benefit of all peoples. God did not begin the world with Israel; however, after the great Flood, and in view of the continuing disobedience of humankind, the Lord did direct himself especially to this people: he created it, when it was no people, in order that it would answer to his purpose. Moreover, it is clear from numerous messianic prophecies that the purpose of Israel's separate existence was not to be found in its continuing existence as such – after all, it was abundantly sinful itself – but in the coming of the Messiah, the One who would come to cleanse Israel and gather the nations. The prophecies that portray the future may not be isolated from all of that. The colours of that painting have been taken from the palette that was available: the land, the city, the people, the vineyard, Carmel, Assyria. The question whether these colours indicate that the future includes a special 'Jewish' future in Palestine should not be answered by a reference to the imagery used, but by drawing on the non-figurative revelation concerning the relative position of Jews and Gentiles. And it is clear from that non-figurative instruction (notably in Romans and Galatians) that all those who have faith in the great Son of Abraham, by this faith are also counted as descendants of Abraham, and share in all the promises to him. Everything that is promised to 'Abraham's seed' in the prophecies, is given to all those who have faith in Christ, to the Jew first, and also to the Gentile.

Whenever we take into account what Genesis 1-12, along with the prophets and apostles, teach us about 'Israel' as 'God's people', we are not substituting a 'spiritual' interpretation for a 'literal' one; rather, we read the literal meaning (including its imagery) as it appears within the context in which the prophets spoke.

Romans 11:25-32 and the fulfilment of prophecy

Following on from the previous section, we still must further consider the oft-quoted passage from Romans 11, in which Paul seems to speak of the mystery of a future conversion of the Jewish people. Doesn't this mystery have great significance for the 'literal' fulfilment of prophecy, one which the Christian church has too hastily 'spiritualized' and annexed for its own purposes? The interpretation of Romans 11 has hermeneutical consequences for numerous passages from the prophets.

In Romans 11:25-32, Paul writes:

> *"Lest you be wise in your own sight, I do not want you to be unaware of this mystery, brothers: a partial hardening has come upon Israel, until the fullness of the Gentiles has come in. And in this way all Israel will be saved, as it is written,*
>
> *'The Deliverer will come from Zion; he will banish ungodliness from Jacob; and this will be my covenant with them when I take away their sins.'*
>
> *"As regards the gospel, they are enemies for your sake. But as regards election, they are beloved for the sake of their forefathers. For the gifts and the calling of God are irrevocable. For just as you were at one time disobedient to God but now have received mercy because of their disobedience, so they too have now been disobedient in order that by the mercy shown to you they also may now receive mercy. For God has consigned all to disobedience, that he may have mercy on all".*

While this passage is often understood as pointing to a future conversion of the whole Jewish nation, there are all kinds of reasons present in these verses that render such an interpretation dubious. We list a few:

1. The passage does not say that Israel will be saved 'in connection with' the coming in of the Gentiles, but 'by way of' this coming in. *In this way* all Israel will be saved.

2. An acceptance of the Gospel by the Jewish people as a whole is not to be expected; for in Romans 9 Paul points out that it is not the natural descendants of Abraham who are 'God's children', but it is the 'children of the promise' who are counted as his offspring (ch 9:8). That is also why he says that *"not all who are descended from Israel belong to Israel"* (ch 9:6).

3. The central theme of Romans 9-11 is in fact election by means of faith that is worked through the preaching. It is through this preaching that God calls his people from both Jews *and* Greeks (ch 9:24-10:13).

4. In Romans 11 this general theme is more closely focused on the relationship between the Jews' unbelief and the conversion of the nations. Does this imply that God has finished with the Jews? Paul responds to this question by showing that the conversion of the Gentiles has the repentance and completion of Israel in view. Gentiles are being grafted into Israel (ch 11:13-24). He describes this as a 'mystery' – not in the sense of 'an unanticipated surprise in the future', but as a 'profound act of God in the present'. This understanding of the word 'mystery' will also be gained by a careful reading of Ephesians 3:1-13 and Romans 16:25-27. This is clear from the fact that Paul's argument in ch 11:25-32 does not conclude with a comforting exhortation to await a future exaltation of the Jewish people, but with an indication that the conversion of the Gentiles is intended to lead the Jews to envy (ch 11:31; 11:11,13-14). This is also clear from ch 11:25, where Paul points to this mystery *"lest you* (Gentiles) *be wise in your own sight"*. Evidently, a prediction concerning the future destiny of the Jews would not have any effect on the Gentile believers' attitude at that time. However, a statement that the completion of Israel would come about by the Gentiles' conversion could well evoke such an attitude among them.

5. If Paul had been certain about a later conversion of the Jews as a whole, he would not have spoken in a conditional sense in ch 11:23: *"And even they, if they do not continue in their unbelief, will be grafted in"*.

For a sound understanding of Romans 11:25, more attention must be given to what Paul says about *'the fullness of the Gentiles coming in'*. What kind of 'coming in' is that? Coming into what? Into the kingdom of heaven? But then, why doesn't he say so? We ought to remember that Paul has just introduced the imagery of wild branches being grafted into a cultivated olive tree. It isn't the Gentiles who are the root, but the root of Israel supports them (ch 11:18). Being grafted into a cultivated stem points to a 'coming in' to another tree. It is through a process of grafting that Gentiles 'come in' to the stem of Israel. That is the context by which the subsequent verse (25) may be understood: a partial hardening has come upon Israel, until the fullness of the Gentiles has come in, and that is how all Israel will be saved.

'All Israel', then, truly is the offspring of Abraham. However, the key point is that this 'all' Israel does not become whole by natural reproduction, but by a Spiritual conversion and grafting. In terms of their ancestry, 'all' Israel consists partly of converted Jews, and partly of the fullness of Gentiles that have been brought in. Jews who have come to Christ *remain* offspring of Abraham, and Gentiles who come to faith *become* offspring of Abraham. That is the mystery of the Gospel: it doesn't write off the old covenant people; rather, it completes the true Israel.

Paul quotes the prophecy of Isaiah. Isaiah had clearly foretold that the Saviour would not come from Athens or from Rome, but from Zion (Isaiah 59:20). Jesus is truly descended from the Jews *'according to the flesh'*(Romans 9:5). And Isaiah had prophesied that God's covenant with Israel was not based on bodily descent, but on the forgiveness of sins (Isaiah 59:20; Jeremiah 31:33-34). This prophecy highlights both the central position of Israel in the covenant, and the starting point for the formation of God's people.

From this perspective, Paul can say in Romans 11:28 that the Jews are *'enemies as regards the Gospel'*: they have rejected the Messiah, and persecuted his people. However, at the same time he can call them *'beloved as regards election'*. Here, Paul does not mean that the entire Jewish people as such are God's chosen people. What he briefly points to here, he has expounded in more detail in ch 9: God chooses his people from among Israel. A remnant will be saved (ch 9:27). Paul himself is one such chosen child of God (ch 11:1-2): there is still a remnant chosen by grace (ch11:5-7).

When we consider this chosen Israel, we see how Israel (in this elect remnant) is still beloved for the sake of the forefathers. God has no regret over his promises to Benjamin; after all, the Benjamite Saul may become an apostle to the world. After all that has been said in Romans 9-11, it is self-evident that the words *'according to election'* in ch 11:28 have a limiting application, while the words *'according to the Gospel'* have a generalizing application. For the moment, the nation of oppressors is regarded separately from the 'elect remnant' (for a comparably generalizing application see ch 9:2-3; 9:31-32; 10:21). And from the other side the 'elect remnant' is viewed as the people who are *'beloved for the sake of the forefathers'* (for this approach, compare ch 9:31 with ch 11:7). When in ch 11:29 Paul says that *'the gifts and calling of God are irrevocable'*, he sees this worked out in the elect remnant, that part of the natural Israelites that believes and is saved.

That remnant exists. At first, Paul had joined in with the stoning of Stephen, but later God had turned him around, and brought him to obedience. In the same way, the obedience of Christians from the Gentiles must be directed to the conversion of disobedient Jews (ch 11:30-31). For God had consigned all to disobedience: not a single person, not a single nation, is able to take pride in its own excellence. And this course of events will lead to the splendour of God's forgiving Gospel: first to the Jews and then to the Gentiles (ch 11:32ff).

Romans 11:25-32 lends no support to a *national* interpretation of Old Testament prophecies that speak about the future of the Israel of God. On the contrary, these verses, together with many other passages from the Old and the New Testament, support the understanding that the interpretation of prophecies concerning the future of Israel must take account of what the Lord has revealed elsewhere about how God forms his people Israel in this world. Such an approach leads to a non-national interpretation.

Isaiah prophesies that *"in the latter days ... the mountain of the house of the Lord shall be established as the highest of the mountains... All the nations shall flow to it ... For out of Zion shall go forth the law, and the word of the Lord from Jerusalem"* (ch 2:1-5). Considering what the mount of Zion looked like in those days, this imagery seems rather incongruous. From the New Testament, it is much clearer that this is about the heavenly Jerusalem, of which its earthly counterpart was a foreshadowing and a reflection. After all, the writer to the Hebrews says: *"we have come to "Mount Zion, to the city of the living God, the heavenly Jerusalem"* (ch 12:22). And he is not the only one to make this application. Paul, too, speaks of the *'Jerusalem that is above'*, *'the mother of us all'* (Galatians 4:25-26; Philippians 3:20). And in the Revelation to John we also read about the heavenly Jerusalem, descending as a fulfilment of Old Testament prophecy (ch 21). On the gates of this city are inscribed the names of the twelve tribes of Israel. The earthly Jerusalem proved to be a foretaste of the heavenly Jerusalem. But lest the Gentiles become wise in their own sight, we read engraved on its gates the names of the forefathers of Israel. And so all Israel will be saved (Revelations 22:3,12). By faith in the Gospel of the apostles of the Lamb, who themselves were elect from Israel (ch 22:14).

The perspective of Scripture determines the interpretation of prophecy! And this leads to an exegesis that is at the same time truly 'literal' and truly 'Spiritual'. This enables us to avoid the pitfalls of an interpretation that isolates letters from the Book, and that, failing to recognize the New Covenant as the fulfilment of prophecy, downgrades it into some kind of an intermezzo before the fulfilment, an interim for the church before the state of Israel is restored.

Prophecy and visions

Many prophecies owe their origin to messages the prophets received directly from God: the Lord told them beforehand what he was planning. Some other prophecies, however, came to the prophets in visions: the seer viewed the future from a distance.

In this way Balaam, *"the man whose eye is opened"*, saw Christ from afar: *"I see him, but not now; I behold him, but not near: a star shall come out of Jacob, and a sceptre shall rise out of Israel; it shall crush the forehead of Moab and break down all the sons of Sheth"* (Numbers 24:17). Before the event, Micaiah the son of Imlah *"saw all Israel scattered on the mountains, as sheep that have no shepherd"*, and the Lord accompanied the vision with a commentary about the imminent death of King Ahab (I Kings 22:17). Daniel and Zechariah saw night visions, and on the island of Patmos the apostle John was allowed to observe *"the things that must soon take place"* (Revelation 1:1).

The writings of these last prophets are often – and too quickly – characterised as 'apocalyptic literature', as if we are dealing with a standard literary form, worked out by each of them in their own fashion, just as one author might choose the form of a fairy tale, and another a ballad. Were this to be so, then we are dealing here with literary fiction: the prophet is composing fictional text. However, one cannot discredit the prophets' claims about what they *really saw* by explaining them away as another fictional form. That can only be done if 'apocalyptic literature' is a well-defined concept – that is certainly not the case – and if it could be shown that the prophets' actual intention was to write fiction. On the contrary, the reverse is true. Daniel's visions greatly terrify him, in a distinctly different manner from the way that an author of fiction might be fascinated by his own material (Daniel 7:28; 18:27; 10:15-19). Zechariah himself really does not know what he is to make of his visions (Zechariah 1:1,19; 2:2; 4:4-5, 11-12; 5:6; 6:4). John is told to come up into heaven (Revelation 4:1), and he knows as little as Zechariah does (7:13-14; 22:8).

For the exegete, it is important to be able to take into account the difference between a prophecy and a vision. Even though these two may be interwoven, there is clearly a difference between what the prophet is told beforehand to *say*, and what he may *see*. With *spoken* revelation, the imagery is often more clearly limited by the time in which it is presented, and the perspective of the prophet who speaks: eternal peace is promised in the context of a time that is marked by swords and pruning-hooks. On the other hand, visions (revelations that are *seen*) are usually much more dominated by realities that are beyond our knowledge: we are looking at things that to us are strange and unfamiliar. Specific elements of the vision may be represented in terms of the familiar: the water of the river is as 'bright as crystal', but the representation as a whole is determined by what can only be seen elsewhere; by things that are hidden from our sight.

From the perspective of heaven, the future looks quite different than it does from the perspective of human history. Of course, we may try to find points of recognition in them. But the 'thousand years' are not a thousand calendar years, and the 'dragon' does not appear in some kind of conventional form. Does this mean that everything presented in a vision is only imaginary, and has nothing to do with something real? We could only draw such a conclusion if reality as we observe it is the only reality that exists. And that is certainly not the case. Numerous realities are unknown to us, even though they may strongly influence our world-view. With the Lord, a thousand years are as one day, and one day as a thousand years. From our perspective, the future has not yet arrived, and we cannot construct some kind of programme about it beforehand: and yet the prophets see things that are still to come, as though they were already present. In a certain sense, in their vision they are truly present already. After all, who knows what is on the other side?

There is nothing wrong then, as an exegete, to be rather puzzled and uncertain when interpreting a vision. But it would be worse if we were to regard reports about other places and times purely as visual expression, and not as a true representation of reality, for then we would be attempting to mirror the vision in our own world-view. In a vision, the reader stands at a window, so to speak, and looks outside. Fortunately, such a reader does not have to know everything in order to see the sun shining, and the clouds rushing by. It is the exegete's task, when interpreting a vision, to help the reader see what is recorded there. A painting can hardly be turned into a piece of written text: similarly, a vision cannot easily be transformed into an informational text. Still, a vision allows us to take in a good deal, and it does lend us a certain perspective. Even if it may not be possible to come to a conclusive and complete exegesis of the passage, since the circumstances of the world of the vision are insufficiently known to us, and are beyond our capacity to investigate.

CHAPTER 6

Discerning the meaning of the text

Who makes meaning?

Throughout the ages the Bible has been used to formulate messages and compose songs for later generations: the reading book was also a songbook and a book of sermons. Whether we think of bringing consolation to the dying, composing a confession, delivering Sunday sermons, or developing ethical and moral rules, the Bible has always been a normative resource for all of these. It is a book of meanings, for later readers as well.

For many in our postmodern age, however, an unbridgeable chasm has grown between the Bible as a reading book from the past, and the meaning these texts might have for our own time. This chasm has become even deeper because of the separation between faith and science, and because of the fragmentation of the text owing to decanonization. For many, there no longer seems to be a credible bridge between the original, historical-literary meanings uncovered by careful exegesis of the text, and later interpretations, an added value, as it were. It is true that, as in earlier times, Bible texts are still used in preparing sermons, but the preacher is much more hesitant to present the text itself as something to be preached about. This holds true, whether the text is used as the basis for a dogmatic or ethical proposition, or whether it serves to provide comfort in times of trial or sorrow. In the minds of many, there is no real connection any more between the meaning of the text itself, and the meaning that is constructed by the hearer: the modern reader makes the best of an ancient, inspiring text, but in and of itself such a text has little or no connection with one's own time or situation. Postmodern readers construct their own meanings from what – for them – has actually become a meaningless piece of text.

The Roman Catholic scholar Christoph Dohmen has made an attempt to portray this modern practice (of separating the meaning of the text itself from the meaning constructed by the hearer) as a variant within the catholic pattern of the church throughout the ages. In a 1992 publication he defended the concept of multifaceted or multiple meanings of a text. Next to the original text, he writes, there is also the need for application of the text in new or changed situations. In this way adjustments in usage and application emerge within the church's tradition, adjustments that are not directly related to the meaning of the text itself, but that come along as unintended effects of the texts upon later readers and listeners (the *Wirkungsgeschichte* of the text). These meanings for the audience can often vary, be they traditional, materialist, feminist or whatever. In a certain sense, readers construct a meaning that speaks to them in their own time and situation as relevant and meaningful.[38]

Dohmen lent legitimacy to this subjective view of the meaning of the text as 'catholic' by describing it as a variation of the concept of the 'fourfold meaning of Scripture' as it was developed in the Middle Ages. This fourfold view of meaning includes, next to the literal sense of text, its allegorical, moral and eschatological meaning. According to Dohmen, the roots of this view go back to the first centuries of the Christian Church, when it had to actualise the Old Testament in a new situation. In a highly multicultural society such as our own, Dohmen argues, it ought to be possible to assign fresh new meanings to old texts, within the protective frameworks of the canon and of tradition.

Is Dohmen correct when he states that already in the Middle Ages the Church regarded the literal meaning of the text as insufficient, and that the Christian church, by developing three additional meanings, intended to ease the reception of texts in later periods and for more modern audiences? There are several reasons why such a portrayal is open to debate.

1. First, already in the 1st century AD the Jewish author Philo of Alexandria produced a spiritual interpretation of the Old Testament

writings that showed many formal resemblances to the spiritualized readings of Moses' Scriptures which emerged within the Christian Church (the latter, of course, viewed from the perspective of the coming of Christ).

2. Second, the author of the epistle to the Hebrews bases his argument for a spiritual reading of the Old Testament from within Scripture itself, and on the basis of the intrinsic structure of the old dispensation; there is no evidence that he has any idea of a model of reinterpretation from a later historical perspective.

3. Third, from the earliest centuries the two-, three- or fourfold model of Scripture meanings was applied to the whole of Scripture, not just to the Old Testament. This shows that the primary intent of this model was not to actualize the Old Testament for later or different ways of thinking, but as an approach to reading Scripture as such.

4. Fourth, efforts have always been made, with varying degrees of success, to show how these other layers of meaning were already implied in the meaning of the texts themselves, or in any case to the events that the texts described. While it is true that these allegorical, ethical and eschatological interpretations aimed to create bridges with their audiences in later periods, the bridgeheads for these efforts were sought in the texts themselves, and not in the perceived 'needs' of later audiences, or in their situational contexts.

The only reasonable conclusion is that a modern view, one that works with plural meanings derived by the hearers within their own time and place, and aiming for a reanimation of an obsolescent text, cannot be regarded as a direct extension of the catholic approach to reading the Bible.

The tradition of twofold or fourfold meaning of Scripture

Having said that, Dohmen's article does invite us to stop and think for a moment about the 'twofold or fourfold meaning' model of Scripture interpretation, as it functioned in the early church, and as it was codified and systematized in the Middle Ages. Revisiting this concept is useful as we reflect on the lasting value that Bible texts might have in a modern (or postmodern) time.[39]

The classic formulation of this concept may be found in the renowned distichon of the Scandinavian Augustine of Dacia (d.1282). For generations of mediaeval students, this poem, written in couplet form, set the hermeneutical standard. It went like this:

> *Littera gesta docet, quid credas allegoria,*
> *Moralis quid agas, quo tendas anagogia.*

It could be translated as:

> *The letter teaches the facts,*
> *allegory what is to be believed;*
>
> *The moral tells what one must do,*
> *eschatology where one must go.*

At first reading, it appears that this distichon lists four separate meanings. On closer examination, however, it becomes clearer that a dual structure dominates, one that in the ancient church was usually characterized as its literal meaning on the one hand, and its spiritual or allegorical meaning on the other. Within the scholastic framework this dual meaning was more precisely systematized, elaborating on sub-aspects of its second, spiritual meaning. It begins with a literal meaning, the *gesta* (the actual events that took place and the words that were spoken: the facts). This leads to what is actually *one* spiritual meaning, which helps us make sense of what these facts and words actually mean to us in later times.

This is clear from the structure of the distichon. It contains a hidden code: faith (*quid credas*), love (*quid agas*) and hope (*quo tendas*). How does one arrive at the literal meaning of the text, in a manner that edifies a spiritual life consisting of faith, love and hope? By considering the events and statements as recorded in the text. A rereading of the text will highlight three facets: *allegoria, ethica et anagogia*. These three are facets of the spiritual life, not of the text. However, they are facets that may be viewed in line with the purpose of the text, namely to serve the edification of the saints. These facets do not flow from the needs or interests of later times, even though they may well be applied to these later concerns.

Evidence that this fourfold meaning is in fact regarded as an elaboration of a literal-spiritual duality is clear from the life's work of the mediaeval Parisian scholar Nicholas of Lyra. His commentaries on the fourfold meaning of Scripture were written in two volumes, not in four: the *Postillae* (the literal meaning) and the *Moralia* (the spiritual sense)!

It is therefore not as simple as Dohmen would have us believe, to exchange the fourfold meaning of the text for a modern multidimensional one. In fact, Christianity has only ever taught a single spiritual meaning, even though it may have been elaborated in multiple ways.[40]

The meaningful world behind the text

Having understood that exegetes were trying to find spiritual meaning (allegory, morality, eschatology) in the text, the question remains: the meaning of what? Of the text? Does the text itself have a double layer? And does this mean that the act of reading the text imposes a double meaning on it, a second meaning imposed upon its original or literal meaning? No, the distichon shows that the interpreter of the text's literal meaning focuses on the text itself, and on the words and events described in it, but that the spiritual explanation of the text draws attention to the *implications of these gesta* (the words and the facts) for a Christian life in faith, hope and love. Nicholas of Lyra makes this point explicitly when he observes that the literal or historical meaning of texts comes to us by way of the *words themselves* (the language) while their threefold spiritual meanings are conveyed in the *matters* indicated by the language.[41] The literal meaning conveys the facts, the wise sayings, and the parables that are being recounted. And the *contents* of these texts convey deeper meanings. Just as Paul says in I Corinthians 10, they are *types*. As he writes in Galatians 4, they point further than just Sarah's tent.

It was Thomas Aquinas who thought extensively about the deepest ground for this spiritual reading of Scripture. Thomas' thought processes in this regard have been described and explained by the Chilean theologian Maximino Arias Reyero.[42] He shows how Thomas, already in one of his earliest commentaries (on the *Sentences of Peter Lombard*), searched for a theological justification of the twofold meaning of Scripture. Thomas presented his most refined summary of this concept later, in his *Summa Theologica*. As he explains it, it is the unity of God and of his plan for the world that also determines the interconnections between his works. The Christian may meditate on these works, drawing hope, learning love, and growing in faith from them. It is Scripture that brings us into contact with these realities of the works of God. Spiritual meaning, then, is not directed primarily to the literal *text*, but to the *matters* that are articulated in it.[43] Exegesis of the text serves to bring the reader to the true *theologia:* the knowledge of and meditation upon who God is, and of his works.

It is precisely at this point that modern Bible scholarship has moved onto another track. While Den Heyer, in his *Bijbels Handboek*, may describe this transition as *'a hopeful moment of birth in true Bible scholarship'*[44], others regard it as the beginning of a drawn-out and debilitating sickness within the field of theology. Rooted as it is in Enlightenment thinking, modernist Bible scholarship has lost the thread that ties together God's *gesta*, his deeds, and as a result the whole unified texture of the canon has fallen into a heap.

Owing to the post-Enlightenment time in which they live, orthodox exegetes now find themselves investing large parts of their scholarship in studies into the literal or historical meaning of the text. Why do they need to go to such trouble? Why does there need to be such painstaking investigation of the life of Christ on earth, and of the work of the apostle Paul, one of the pioneers of the Gospel? To defend a sacred text? Not really. Much more to ensure that the path to the *gesta* (the works of God), and, via the *gesta,* the path to Biblical dogmatics, ethics and eschatology contained in the *gesta,* remains open.

The doctrine of a twofold meaning of Scripture is in reality the doctrine of a unified meaning of Scripture: Scripture really does mean what it says! It truly does deal with realities! And that is why meditation on the facts and on the works of God is a self-evident consequence, unavoidably bound up with a reading of the literal and historical meaning of the text. Broadly, therefore, we may speak of dual meanings of Scripture, the literal and the spiritual meaning, even though we are actually dealing with a single, unified meaning, and the consequences that flow from this meaning for our faith, our morality, and our expectation for the future. In other words, we are dealing with the text, and with the way it changes or converts us.

The Bible is full of texts that we may use to confess, to live by, to sing, and to hope in, for these texts give us a view of the heights of the works and words of God, which are one and the same. And it is precisely because we can distinguish between the *meaning* of the text itself and the *reality* signified by the text, that the person of the exegete is part of the process.

Of course: the Bible is the Word of God, and it speaks for itself. However, as much as the Scriptures were given by holy men, driven by the Spirit of God, this does not set aside the fact that we are to search the Scriptures, with prayer and meditation, in order to be able and willing to see the depths and heights of what is written in them. That is why the poet of Psalm 119 writes: *"Open my eyes, that I may behold wondrous things out of your law"* (v.18). Following the path from exegesis to confession, sermon and song does not just happen by itself. Each reader must use the stairway of the text to be able, in faith, to set one's feet upon the heights of God's great works. It is only through faith that this inspiring panorama appears to the community of believing readers, and to each reader individually.

Does this mean that each reader may spiritually discern the meaning of the text through independently subjective construction, and that there is no need or place for an exegesis of the text itself? That is not so. While it is true that it is only the Spirit of God who enables us to understand and accept the things of God (II Corinthians 2:12-16, see also II Peter 1:19-21), the Spirit unlocks our understanding by means of the correction and comfort of Scriptures, prophecy that does not come by one's own interpretation. The works of God include the sending of prophets, apostles, and teachers of Scripture. It is only in following in their footsteps that we will find the road to the heights of Sinai and the Mount of Olives.

From Bible to songbook

We cannot get away from it: the profit we reap for our own assurance, our joy and our hope comes to us through the birth pangs of exegesis. Of course, there is much more to it: meditation, spirituality, respect for our tradition, etc, but for the moment we will limit ourselves to the text as our gateway to confession, song and sermon. And here we will often run into a practical problem. For isn't it the case that the literal, historical meaning of the text, rather than opening the way to making connections with our own time, in fact gets in the way? Doesn't it seem that exegesis of the literal or historical meaning creates a distance for us in our 21st century experience of the world, and creates a blockage between ourselves and the text of the Bible? At first sight, it appears that this distance forces us into a detour. Granted, finding the road back to the time of the text is illuminating; it removes problems in and around the text, but the removal of such barriers to our understanding is not yet enough to generate the spark that jumps across to our song, life and sermon. Instead, it seems to take us further away from home, further from our own time, with its own issues and its own problems.

Still, this path back to the text is indispensable. First of all, as a means of accountability: if the interpretation of the Bible that we derive in our time and context is to be legitimate, it ought to be found in the text itself, and in the reality that the text portrays. Second, a sound and robust exegesis of the text itself protects us from mystical or postmodern arbitrariness, in which texts are quoted and applied out of context, just because they sound right. Third, proper exegesis helps us not to be taken captive by our own questions or concerns; rather, it teaches us to ask questions that fit with the text itself.

Still, as praiseworthy as this path back to the text itself may be, is it really a path that we *can* follow? Doesn't the text, on its way to making meaning for us in our context, sometimes die an untimely death? What gain is there for us in reading about the distribution of tribal territories in Joshua: a patchwork of traditions? What could we learn from Galatians: a letter written for a specific situation that would not occur today? Are those ancient texts really all that suitable for the great narrative, and for a later era?

In confronting these questions, it is important that we – again! – realize that we are dealing with texts found in the Bible, in other words within the totality of what God has said and done. *Littera gesta docet* – the letter teaches the facts! The Bible is a collection of writings by men, a product of 'holy men' (II Peter 1:21, NKJV), and yet these Scriptures are one, united by the voice and the pathway of the Eternal One. The names of the streets may be old, but their aroma is holy, and it has not dissipated! The book transports us into the fellowship of the saints. The texts within the text are, as it were, images of the saints of the worldwide church. They are stations along the *via dolorosa,* a gallery of statues lining the triumphal avenue of the Gospel. They are the threads from which God has woven the cloth of his works. The texts are the doors and windows that open a view to the wide field of a history that is greater than what is usually apparent, a history that is full of mystery. Exegesis is the entry and the passage into the worldwide communion of saints, on high with Christ in heaven, and down below here on earth. We may progress from faith to faith, from the faith of the early martyrs to our own faith in modern 21st century Western society.

The patchwork of conquest and land allotment that we find in Joshua is one small step on the way to the new earth: a place and time where nations will live together, peaceably and without border conflicts. We learn how these small steps have been taken, here below. The clumsy symbol portrayed in Joshua points to a higher and better inheritance. And a heated letter, written for a specific situation in a specific Celtic community (the Galatians), shows us something of the enduring sentiment of the Gospel, and something of the human emotion in which this sentiment is always expressed here on earth.

That is how we can see, right through the curtain of the text, the person of the apostle. We recognize his scars, and we feel his longings. He writes a few words. They light up. The reader leans forward: *"But God's Word is not chained!"* (II Tim 2:9). And indeed, there they go: Timothy, Silas, Erastus. Unchained, they go into the world to preach the Word. The text is clear. But it must have taken great self-denial for Paul to write these words while he himself was chained in prison. How selflessly he writes them! What lies behind these words is quite profound. In Paul's eyes, you can read his soul, and in them is reflected the Spirit of Christ in his heart (II Corinthians 3). Here too, the text gives us a perspective, one that Christians can learn from, one to take an example from, and to be encouraged by.

By way of the text, praying Christians find their way to the reality that really matters in our world. That is why we must purposefully grasp the door handle of the text, but not cling to it. In other words, do not just read the *text*, but believe in and meditate on the *realities* portrayed in the text: they are part of the Bible, and part of the catholic, undoubted Christian faith. Dare to dream, together with all the saints. That is why it's good to read more than just the Bible. To read, in communion with all the saints. Their confessions, their martyrs' testimonies teach us to follow the way, through the text, to faith, hope and love. Augustine, Thomas and Spurgeon are our readers in the church. It is good that we, as we read, remember those who went before us.

Knowing this helps us to avoid getting wrapped up in the short-sightedness of the moment, and trapped in the straitjacket of current fads of our cultural and church history. The Bible is meant to lift us out of that as we read it. Modern 21st century Westerners have much to gain from entering, through the gates of these ancient texts, terrain that they have long forgotten. After all, the earthly text of every prophet and seer is a text that carries us back into communion with the saints of earlier times, and at the same time into communion with the Church above, with all the saints, and with the Father and the Son. In this way, a text given to us to *read* also becomes a text from which to *sing*. It is not for nothing that the Bible concludes with the songbook of Revelation. Often, a song expresses the realities of a text far more profoundly than an exegete could ever do. For a voice speaks, but an echo resounds!

CHAPTER 7
A contested book

In our century, the unchallenged authority of Scripture is no longer the starting point for most people's approach to the Bible. Its writings are no longer accepted as they come to us, but only insofar as they can withstand the test of our criticism or be received on the wavelength of our own experience. This uninhibited approach to Scripture is seemingly legitimized by what is commonly known as "modern Bible scholarship". Since much of this criticism of Scripture presents itself as having 'scholarly' or 'scientific' authority, any challenges to such criticism are often *a priori* dismissed as being 'unscientific'. However, it is just at this point that careful reflection is anything but superfluous. Can we truly regard the liberties taken with Scripture and the canon as the attainments of greater scholarly insight, by which Christians are freed from superficial or naïve belief in what the Bible says? Or is there another perspective?

This chapter does not mean to occupy itself with all kinds of concrete questions that are raised by modern exegetes, questions that require concrete answers. In the pages that follow, we will instead examine the climate in which such discussions take place. To those who accept the position that a free and critical attitude to Scripture is a genuine fruit of true scholarship, one that is based on objective facts, unfettered by prejudice or presupposition, anyone who wishes to challenge this critical approach to the Bible can and will be *a priori* dismissed as someone who is out-of-step with the times, someone who wishes to rigidly hold on to and preserve old-fashioned and unscientific points of view. A critique of Bible criticism is regarded as something for people who have been born in the wrong era, people who would have been better off living in the 18th or 19th century. Such a view is, however, destructive for a true discussion of the issue.

In this regard, it is instructive to go back into history. Did criticism of the canon really first arise from modern scholarship? Might such criticism not actually have much older roots, and simply reappear in our time in another, more contemporary manifestation? If this is the case, it doesn't mean that we can simply dismiss the discussion, and stop our investigations. However, it does free us from the frustrating portrayal of Scripture criticism as modern and scientific, and of faith in Biblical revelation as naïve and simplistic.

The historical survey presented in this chapter has four parts. First, we will pay some attention to the period that preceded the determination and canonization of written revelation. Next, we will examine the era in which Biblical revelation functioned in a written, canonized form. Then we will provide a sketch of the self-portrayal of modern, critical Bible scholarship, and an overview of its historical development. Finally, we will discuss the attitude that is fitting for our own reading of the Bible.

"Did God really say...?"

Criticism of God's revelation is as old as Paradise itself: it stems from Satan's first attack on humankind as God created it. The serpent's first question to the Woman was this one: *"Did God really say that you must not eat from any tree in the garden?"* – a suggestive question, with an undertone critical of God himself. And this criticism of God is immediately followed by criticism of his revelation, in the serpent's subsequent comment: *"You will not certainly die ... for God knows that when you eat from it your eyes will be opened, and you will be like God, knowing good and evil"* (Genesis 3:1-5). This beginning sets the stage for a centuries-long continuation.

In his hatred of God, and of God's love for mankind, Satan throws all kinds of weapons into the battle: false doctrine, worldly ways of living, persecution, and discouragement. All of these weapons, however, are most often sharpened on the same whetstone: criticism of God's revelation. That is how everything else is undermined: for who would have the courage to build their lives on something that is unsteady and doubtful? How can a word that is contested and uncertain serve as a cornerstone for human activity?

Throughout history, we consistently see God's continuing revelation besieged by gnawing criticism. When God, through Moses, delivers his people, and gives them life-giving laws, these laws are undermined by grumbling: *"Has the Lord indeed spoken only through Moses? Has he not spoken through us also?"* (Numbers 2:20). When the Lord speaks solemn words through Jeremiah, in order to save his people from destruction, and when he causes these words to be recorded for king Jehoiakim, we see the king cut page after page from the scroll and throw them into a fire, discarding them as not worth listening to (Jeremiah 36:23). Jesus' majestic authority over demons, so impressive to the multitudes, is desecrated by the teachers of the law, through their dismissive suggestion that he has allied himself to Beelzebub, the prince of demons. (Mark 3:22).

Christ himself once emphatically exposed the roots of this unrelenting hostility and criticism. On one occasion, his enemies dismiss his revelation of the Father as evidence that he is a Samaritan, and demon-possessed (John 8:42). Jesus replies: *"Why do you not understand what I say? It is because you cannot bear to hear my word. You are of your father the devil, and your will is to do your father's desires. He was a murderer from the beginning, and has nothing to do with the truth, because there is no truth in him. When he lies, he speaks out of his own character, for he is a liar and the father of lies"* (John 8:43-44). These serious and harsh words are spoken to people who think of themselves as standing in a tradition of faith. And it is a warning for us, that we may realize that not everyone accepts God's revelation as self-evident. God gives his revelation in a world full of the smoke of battle. Toxic gases can so easily overcome us, rendering us unable – or even unwilling – to hear what God is truly saying. From the moment that God reveals himself, there will always be a massive counteracting force, intent on covering up or obscuring this revelation by any means possible.

The forms such criticism might take will vary, but several chief forms stand out:

a. Criticism of the *source* of the revelation. At the actual moment that the Lord was busy performing his great deeds in the world, it was often hard to deny the factual reality of these events. Pharaoh cannot possibly ignore the signs Moses performs. However, he does attempt to find an explanation that places the origin of these signs, not in the almighty hand of God, but in the magician's skills of the mighty man

Moses. After all, cannot his own magicians accomplish similar things? Even this way of escape, however, is cut off: from the third plague on, Pharaoh's magicians stand powerless. Dismayed, they admit: *"This is the finger of God!"* (Exodus 8:18-19). We note a similar attempt to sidestep the force of God's revelation when the Jewish leaders ascribe Jesus' miracles to a satanic origin (Beelzebub), while failing to draw the same conclusion when their own followers drive out demons (Luke 11:18-20). Jesus reminds the Jews that they now have no option but to see the *'finger of God'* in his actions (Luke 11:20).

b. Criticism of the *reality* of the revelation. When an extended period of time elapses between the work of God and the time in which one lives, it becomes easier to cast doubts on the story: perhaps it didn't really happen. The event becomes a tale, and the tale is no longer believed, so that the reality of the history in which God reveals himself is thrown into doubt. In this way Sennacherib, in his contemptuous diatribe before the people of Jerusalem, questions whether it really was the Lord who led his people out of Egypt (Isaiah 36:18ff). And when after the earthquake on Easter morning the fleeing guards have recovered from their fright, the Jewish Council spreads the lie that Jesus' disciples had stolen his body. They want to sweep the reality of Jesus' resurrection under the carpet, and ignore the consequences of its revelation (Matthew 28:11-15). Already in his second epistle, Peter is forced to confront the accusations of people who think that the apostles are following cleverly invented fables (II Peter 1:16).

c. Criticism of the *authority* of revelation. Even if one does not actually deny the divine origin or reality of revelation, one can still undermine it. By its very nature, the revelation of God calls for acceptance, faith and obedience. That is because it is the revelation of *God* to his creatures. This authority, however, can be weakened. That happens when false prophets attempt to stand next to the true prophet, and demand equal attention and respect for their entirely different message. That is how the false prophet Hananiah undermines the word of Jeremiah, when he pulls the yoke off his neck and says: *"Thus says the* LORD*: Even so will I break the yoke of Nebuchadnezzar king of Babylon from the neck of all the nations within* *two years"* (Jeremiah 28:11). And when the prophet Micaiah foretells King Ahab's demise, Zedekiah the son of Chenaanah strikes him on the cheek, and says: *"How did the Spirit of the LORD go from me to speak to you?"* (I Kings 22:24). The apostle Paul, too, had to confront people who presented themselves as apostles, as angels of light, in order to diminish his revelation and undermine respect for what he said (II Corinthians 11:13-15; 12:11-21).

Today, we may still expect this kind of criticism of divine revelation, criticism that has pursued the Word of God in all kinds of ways from the very beginning, criticism brought to bear against the *written text* of revelation, the Bible. It did not, however, begin with criticism of *Scripture* itself; no, it is criticism of *revelation* of which Scripture criticism is the offspring.

"They are only human documents!"

Criticism of the New Testament in the first centuries of the present era has its roots in criticism of the written text of the Old Testament during the centuries before. To begin with, pagans, in their aversion to the Jewish people, criticized the contents of the Book these people lived by. The Jewish 'Bible' was dismissed as a document originating in the minds of a ragtag mob of leprous pariahs, expelled from Egypt, that was intended to bolster their self-image (the pagan historian Tacitus, who lived early in the 2nd century AD, still spoke disparagingly of Jews in these terms). Pagans were especially critical of Jewish dietary regulations, and of the Jews' tendency to separate themselves from mainstream society. The Jewish writer Josephus, a slightly earlier contemporary of Tacitus, attempted to refute such criticism in his *Contra Apionem*, as well as in his more extensive and more positive accounts in his *Jewish Antiquities* and *The Jewish War*.

However, it was not only from the side of pagan writers that Moses and the Prophets had to endure criticism. A challenge concerning the *extent* of the Scriptures also came from another quarter. The Samaritans obstinately refused to accept the Psalms of David, any of the works of Solomon, or any of the prophets, as divine Scriptures. They presumed to have a better grasp of God's revelation by restricting their acceptance to the Pentateuch, and by favouring 'Mosaic' Shechem above 'Davidic' Jerusalem as the designated place of worship (cf John 4:20). From another direction, adherents of some apocalyptic circles cherished, next to the Law and the

Prophets, certain additional secret revelations by Enoch or Baruch. In this way, both the *content* and the *extent* of the Old Testament Scriptures were already subjected to pressure and criticism before the coming of Christ.

What we see happening to the Scriptures of the New Covenant at the beginning of the Christian era actually runs parallel to this earlier development. Here too we are confronted with criticism of both their *extent* and their *content*.

The *content* of the Gospels was contested most notably by *pagan* critics. Just as Josephus opposed the claims of Apion in the first century AD, so Origen did in opposition to the pagan philosopher Celsus in the second. In his *Alèthès Logos* ("The True Word", c. 175 AD) Celsus had attacked the Gospels. How could one exalted truth possibly be chopped up among four gospels, each different from all the others? Celsus regards Jesus as no more than a product of his own time; magic arts from Egypt had somehow given rise to Jesus' miracles, and the typically Hellenistic veneration of people as gods had led to Jesus' followers endowing him with divine attributes.

During the 3rd and 4th centuries AD it was especially the Neoplatonists and the Manicheans who, in their efforts to restore pagan ways of thinking and living, entered into a direct confrontation with Christianity, which in their view was a symptom of a decaying culture. In this manner, the Neoplatonist Porphyrius (b.232 AD), claimed to identify numerous places in which the Gospels were mutually contradictory. He also pointed to what in the 20th century was described as *"Parusieverzögerung"* (the delayed Second Coming). Porphyrius argued that Jesus' words about his imminent return were not fulfilled as predicted, and their failure to eventuate was evidence of the inaccuracy of the Gospel statements. Emperor Julian the Apostate who, in the second half of the 4th century AD, after having been brought up as a Christian, turned away to Neoplatonic paganism, wrote extensively against Christians, those 'Galileans'. He reconstructed a kind of evolutionary history of the Christian faith: in his account Jesus' identification as God is explained as a later Johannine addition to a history that began with a purely human teacher, as originally portrayed by the other evangelists.

Around the same time, and not without reason, the ex-Platonist Augustine wrote a volume that was especially devoted to countering the claim that the

Gospels contradicted each other. His unfinished *De consensu evangelistarum* ('Concerning the consensus of the evangelists') demonstrates how relevant the criticism of the Gospels and the resistance to such criticism was in the early centuries of the Christian church. The content of the Gospel was under attack by means of criticism of the Scriptures in which this Gospel was recorded.

During these same centuries, the *extent* of the New Testament canon also came under fire. This came chiefly from the side of heretics who had divergent views concerning the truth of revelation. From one side, the side of the gnostics, great value was attached to all kinds of writings that were placed next to the New Testament. Just as Jewish apocalyptic circles nurtured various secret revelations, so gnostic groups cherished a secret knowledge of aeons, human and cosmic. Around the end of the 2nd century AD, Irenaeus went to great lengths to expose these gnostics and their supposedly 'secret revelations' in his *Adversus Haereses* ("Against Heresies").

From the other side, over against what was actually an expansion of the canon, a certain formal reduction could also be observed, most notably with Marcion, around the middle of the 2nd century. It was the Marcionites who, proceeding from a certain 'enlightened' conception of God, first arrived at a critical evaluation and a substantial reduction of the New Testament canon (see also Chapter 1). The *form* that this Marcionite reduction took was very specific. However, in later centuries the same *approach* would frequently reappear. Their starting point was their idea that the eternal God is far exalted above all that is earthly. He is even more highly exalted than the 'creator god', the demiurge who created the world, and who in the Old Testament was active under the name Lord (Yhwh). As the Marcionites taught, it was Jesus who first revealed the *supreme* God, and who taught that he was the embodiment of love and grace: human affects such as wrath and sadness were foreign to him. Faith unites people with him, and lifts us above the created world of the demiurge, the world to which heaven and the angels also belong. Proceeding from this conception of God, Marcion also rejected the Old Testament: to him, that part of the Bible had a function only insofar as it provided a sounding board for the more recent revelation of the Gospel. In addition, Marcion retained only those parts of the New Testament that fit this conception: the gospel of Luke and ten of Paul's epistles. The apostle Paul, and Luke, the evangelist most closely associated with him, were supposed to have presented the clearest distinction between the Law as promulgated by the demiurge (the Old Testament) and the Gospel. Christian writers towards the end of the second century AD, led by Tertullian and his *Adversus Marcionem* (against Marcion), forcefully opposed this mutilation of the canon, this carved image of God, with the result that in the end the Marcionite counter-church could not prevail.

This Scripture criticism eventually compelled the early Church to determine with increasing precision and by general agreement which books were to be recognized as authoritative and given by Christ. In the course of time this establishment of the canon became such a firm given that there was less and less room for criticism concerning its extent. The canon of Scripture assumed the position of an established fact. Even in the 20th and 21st centuries, those who from all sides want to chip away at the canon, and wish to retain only scattered portions as authentic and religiously significant, would not contemplate replacing the complete Bible with an 'alternative' or 'purged' version.

On the surface, it may appear that the Bible is now universally accepted in its current form and extent. In reality, however, a *third* form of Scripture criticism has arisen in recent centuries, a mixture of criticism of both its *content* and its *extent*. This is criticism of the *authority* of Scripture.

We characterize this kind of criticism as a mixed form. In common with criticism of the *extent* of the canon, it comes from the side of those who regard themselves as Christian theologians. At the same time, it shares the criticism of the *content* of the Bible with ancient pagan criticism, be it in Christian guise. Christianity as such is not the target of this Scripture criticism, and formally, the extent of the canon is not challenged either. Hence, this approach has the appearance of being less harmful than the criticism of pagans or heretics during the period of the early church. However, in reality this criticism of (parts of) the canon acts as a woodworm in both Christianity itself and its canon.

For what is happening here? Reverence for the revelation of God is hollowed out from the inside, with the result that the foundations of the Christian faith fall victim to decay. A distinction is made between a 'formal canon' and a 'material canon'. The *formal* canon is described as the Bible as it has been received throughout the history of the Christian church, since ancient times. The *material* canon is limited to whatever is assigned a degree of religious authority within this formal canon. The 'real' canon, then, is to be found *within* the formal canon, and can only be further determined through critical theological scholarship. As common as this turn of phrase 'a canon within the canon' may have become, we should still regard it as a deceptive playing with words. In fact, it cannot be more than a play on words: after all, the word 'canon' is used with a variety of diverging meanings. And this is no innocent game: even with the best of intentions it cannot be anything other than deceptive. For the starting point of the argument is masked. After all, the starting point of the concept of the 'canon' is the acceptance of divine authority in an established written revelation. While the term 'canon' is still used, its starting point is erased: after all, a 'canon within the canon', one that arises from human analysis and critical evaluation, can never be a canon that comes to us from outside, by divine authority. Anyone who carves up or mutilates a human body, while claiming that he is looking for the 'person within the person', has lost his respect for the humanity of that person, and has replaced it with the tyranny of one's own conception of humanity.

The search for the so-called 'material canon' can always be justified with an appeal to certain discrepancies that may be observed within or around the text of the Bible. Old soldiers never die! The same objections that were already raised by the enemies of the Jews and the opponents of Christianity in ancient times are simply resurrected. Seeming contradictions between the various gospels, perceived resemblances with other ancient religions, theological 'divergences' within Scripture, conflicting scientific or historical evidence, elements that are deemed unacceptable to later readers, etc, etc, all of these are brought forward. Whereas in earlier times the aim of all of the arguments was to refute Jewish or Christian beliefs, today's 'evidence' is used to uphold the appearance of a canon while removing its essence. Scripture is allowed its place, while 'what is written' is subjected to fierce criticism: faith cannot survive where such abstractions prevail.

And still, it is true: without faith, no one can steer a steady course. But who can hold to such a course if we are expected to steer by a 'compass within the compass'?

Reading by one's own light

Modern historic-critical Bible scholarship operates within an entirely different perspective from the one that we, proceeding from revelation itself, have described above. And that is to be expected. In a manner of speaking, we must make a 180-degree turn to discover how this scholarship sees itself, and with what kind of self-portrayal it feels most comfortable.

We provide two quotations, which could easily be supplemented by numerous similar statements drawn from a variety of other publications. In his *Bijbels Handboek*, Den Heyer writes:

> *"The great change in the interpretation of Biblical writings did not take place during the Reformation, but some centuries later, under the influence of a movement that in European culture was commonly described as 'the Enlightenment'. It is no exaggeration to characterize this movement as a 'Copernican upheaval'. During the 19th century historical-critical Bible scholarship slowly but surely gained ground, and this development has had profound consequences for theology. In increasing measure, exegetes began to realize that the Bible, from beginning to end, was written by people."*[45]

And earlier, Kümmel expressed it quite bluntly this way:

> *"Before the second half of the 19th century one could not really speak of New Testament scholarship in the strict sense of the word. It could only be acknowledged as such from the moment that (in conjunction with the theology of the Enlightenment) the New Testament was recognized as an independent historical entity, separate from the Old Testament scholarship, and when the New Testament, freed from any particular dogmatic or confessional presuppositions, became the object of scholarly investigation. Proceeding from presuppositions arrived at in the second half of the 18th century, 19th century scholars laid the foundations upon which the scholarly study of the New Testament in the 20th century has been built."*[46]

Analysis of a self-portrait

This self-portrait displays a number of remarkable features, which we will summarize and briefly comment on:

a. *Scholarship*. This hallmark is used in such a manner that everything that departs from modern Bible scholarship – in reality, almost everything that was carried out in the centuries prior to the 18th – is denounced as 'unscholarly'. Now that is quite a sweeping and rigorous dismissal. Kümmel somewhat qualifies this assessment by speaking of '*scholarship in the strict sense of the word*'[47]. But then who decides what is '*strict* scholarship'? Are there graduations in what is or is not 'strict' scholarship? Fortunately, by reading between the lines we can work out what Kümmel really means. In his view, the 'strictness' of such scholarship is determined by separation between the Old and the New Testaments, and by the degree to which it is freed from any dogmatic or confessional presuppositions. At first sight, this appears to be quite neutral and objective, but on further examination it emerges that, under the guise of methodological rigour of scholarly research, certain points of departure, specifically dogmatic ones, are in fact excluded from such scholarly activity. After all, isn't it entirely possible that these excluded points of departure are quite appropriate, and fit very well, within the framework of such study? In the pursuit of methodical, scholarly study, it is impossible to avoid points of departure: what is required is careful and continuous consideration of whether the chosen and/or adopted points of departure are appropriate to the object of study, or might perhaps need to be modified in keeping with the objective of the study. In practice, what Kümmel does is to 'freeze' the presupposition that the Old and New Testaments are two separate and independent entities, and that the orthodox confession concerning the nature of the Scriptures is incorrect. Such a confessional point of departure is *a priori* set aside as invalid. Anyone who might still wish to challenge this assumption is labelled as 'not engaging in scholarship in the strict sense of the word'. The real question in this scholarly activity, however, is not whether the church *had* certain dogmatic or confessional points of departure – it did – but whether these points of departure were correct. And the scholarly question is not whether the Old and New Testaments were sometimes interpreted in relation to each other – they were – but whether this was rightly done. Kümmel excludes these questions from scholarly examination, and in doing so his own activity, just as that of many others, is *not* 'scholarly, in the strict sense of the word'. Since in the name of 'scholarship' much orthodox Bible interpretation is silenced, it is of crucial importance to clearly discern that this 'scholarship' is based on the dogmatic presupposition that the Scriptures may not under any circumstances be accepted on their own authority as the revelation of God. This presupposition *a priori* limits the field of Bible scholarship in an unacceptable way, and it wrongly positions itself as 'strictly scholarly' in opposition to the work that scholars carried out in earlier and later centuries.

b. *Neutrality*. By eliminating dogmatic or confessional points of departure, it appears that it is possible to reach a position of neutrality. However, Kümmel himself demonstrates that this is illusory. After all, he makes reference to the *presuppositions* of modern Bible scholarship, as these have been derived in the second half of the 18th century. And he asserts that these presuppositions ('*Voraussetzungen*') arose in close connection with the theology of the Enlightenment. The appearance is often created that modern Bible scholarship is neutral and free of presuppositions ('*voraussetzungslos*'), and that it is therefore superior to believing, confessionally governed Bible scholarship. The reality is, however, that one dogmatic presupposition (the orthodox persuasion) has been exchanged for another dogmatic presupposition (that of the Enlightenment). Much would be gained if this were more openly acknowledged, and the pretence of neutrality was set aside. The true contrast is not between obsolete ('unscholarly') Bible research on the one hand, and modern ('scholarly') study of the Bible on the other, but between a Biblical faith in the providence of God, and the theistic elimination of God from this world.

c. *Restraint*. Where in the past the Old and New Testaments were approached as the unified and interconnected revelation of God, modern practice exercises a supposed 'restraint' in relation to its object of study. The Old Testament, originating in a different period from the New, is now regarded as a separate entity. This quasi-restraint in relation to separate 'historical' entities is in fact a highly qualitative intervention in the object of study as it presents itself. From of old, the Old and New Testaments have been approached as a unity because they have proved to be *internally* interrelated. To ignore this interrelationship with an appeal to their different time of origin is just as nonsensical as to separate the study of the roots and flowers of plants, because the flower has grown later, and is therefore to be regarded as being an 'independent, historically separate entity'. This kind of 'restraint' *a priori* cuts the object of examination in two!

All kinds of analyses, however, cannot negate the reality that in the last two centuries many people simply *live* by this self-portrait: this is how they want to see themselves. Here, we are up against a deeper layer in the history of scholarly activity: there are forces and powers at work that might not be logically defensible, but are still effective. The Bible speaks of *'a strong delusion'* (see II Thessalonians 2:11,12). Such powerful delusions cannot be resisted and dispelled by means of reasoning and refutation alone. Still, a great deal is already gained when the spell of the claimed 'strictly scholarly character' of modern Bible scholarship is broken.

Analysis of an historical account.

Many Christians accept the thought that we, owing to the insights of modern Bible scholarship, have no choice but to adopt a different view concerning the origin and significance of the Old and New Testaments. Less common is the realization that in reality, it is actually the other way around. Modern Bible scholarship *itself* is the product of an altered view of the authority of the canon. This altered view is able to show the changes that occur when Bible scholarship no longer proceeds from the assumption of the authority of Scripture, but that is not in itself proof that should lead us to relinquish our faith in the authority of Scripture. The elaboration of a point of departure does not in itself supply proof that the point of departure is correct! Of course, this also applies to Bible scholarship that *does* accept the divine authority of Scripture. It would be difficult to argue that Bible-believing scholarship in and of itself compels us to return to an older, orthodox confession concerning the Bible. The difference, however, is that the church does not in any way base its faith on 'the outcomes of Bible-believing scholarship', while from the other side the call frequently resounds to "let go of a confessional acceptance of Scripture" on the grounds of *'the* outcomes of modern Bible scholarship'. Since that is the current state of affairs, it would be useful to subject the development of this 'modern Bible scholarship' to closer examination. This section of the present chapter aims to provide a brief and somewhat fragmentary overview of the historical development of 'modern Bible scholarship' as a whole. The purpose of this overview is to show that this negative view of the authority of the canon is the driving and dominant force behind much of this modern scholarship, that this view is foundational for its whole structure, and that it necessarily leads to its predetermined findings and conclusions.

This does, however, present one difficulty. Anyone who engages in historical study, no matter how brief or fragmentary, must do justice to nuances and variations. The picture is never just black-and-white; it will always contain many shades of grey. These could easily be overlooked or removed if we limited or reduced an historical overview to a few dominant features, which would then purport to show that modern Bible scholarship is dominated by an *a priori* position concerning the authority of the canon. In order to avoid the risk of presenting a distorted and oversimplified portrayal within the limited scope of this chapter, we will take the following approach: we present a brief outline of the three most significant fields of study within modern Bible scholarship. While this historical overview will include aspects that may not be directly relevant, it will on the other hand keep this overview from being too schematic. After a birds-eye-view exploration of these three main areas of study, we present a concluding summary, with special attention for the most important focus of this chapter.[48]

The study of the world in which the Bible had its origin

Throughout the ages, there was never a time in which interest in the period when the Saviour lived on earth, or in the world in which the Gospel began its advance, was lacking. This interest, however, took root in especially fertile soil during the centuries of the Renaissance and the rise of Humanism, when there was a rapid increase in scholarly attention for classical texts and the ancient cultures from which they arose. From the 15th century onwards, there was a marked growth in interest in the historical setting of the New Testament.

Shared interest in a field of study, however, does not necessarily guarantee shared outcomes. This would become evident in due course. After all, it makes a big difference whether we study the world of the New Testament in order to better understand God's revelation, or in order to track down the supposed cradle and the substrate of New Testament writings. Initially there did not seem to be much evidence of a divergent perspective, even though in hindsight it could be said that the motivation for this line of inquiry was different for the humanists than it was for the reformers. However, it was not until later that this divergence became clear across the board, when other influences began to exert themselves, leading to a growing divide between those who studied the world of the New Testament from an evolutionary model of the development of Christianity on the one hand, and those who examined this world from the perspective of faith in God's revelation in Jesus Christ and the apostolic witness on the other.

In the periods before and immediately after the great Reformation, the study of the world of the New Testament was based almost exclusively on literary sources: written texts of a certain level (produced by philosophers, historians, poets and religious leaders). This led to a focus in the research of these ancient texts that was directed predominantly at the question whether these texts displayed parallels with the New Testament. Such parallels might be literary or linguistic, enabling clearer understanding of word usage, or of the meaning of words and phrases found in the Bible. Alternatively, these parallels might be historical, clarifying specific events and situations. The study of these various kinds of parallels in ancient Jewish literature was brought together in the work of John Lightfoot (*Horae Hebraicae et Talmudicae in quattor evangelista 1658-78*). The fact that this massive four-volume work was published and circulated in the English language led to it being very well-known and influential. During the 20th century, it was elaborated and superseded by the work of Paul Billerbeck. Stimulated and assisted by his fellow scholar Hermann Strack, Billerbeck compiled an exhaustive compendium of all possible parallels from ancient Jewish sources found in every book of the New Testament. In addition, he wrote a number of monographs on New Testament topics, in which he digested the great amount of material that he had gathered.[49] Parallels from ancient Greek and Roman writers were compiled by the well-known Dutch scholar Hugo de Groot in his *Annotationes in Novum Testamentum* (1641, ff.). A further synthesis and compilation of this work was produced by Johann Jakob Wettstein.[50] Up to the present day, these works have remained the standard resource for all kinds of ancient Jewish and pagan parallel texts. The project *Corpus Hellenisticum Novi Testamenti*, (begun in Utrecht in 1964) aims to be a replacement for Wettstein, but this gigantic project has up till now only produced a number of preparatory studies of the parallels found in a limited number of classical writers.

During the 19th and 20th centuries, the study of the world of the New Testament gained a renewed impetus through the incorporation of the results of archaeological research. This was especially significant for the study of the Old Testament. Gradually, however, it has become increasingly clear that, the well-known adage notwithstanding, the stones themselves do not speak. In the absence of accompanying textual material, by far the greatest number of archaeological findings themselves remain mute. On the contrary, it is precisely because of recent discoveries of *written texts,* and because of the accompanying increase of written source material from antiquity, that archaeological data from this period has become more significant. This is not just because of the increase in the *quantity* of textual material itself, but especially because *different kinds* of texts have now become available: royal inscriptions, commercial archives, and large amounts of all kinds of other non-literary texts in the papyri. Aspects of daily life that did not receive any attention in classical literature were now revealed. This was significant for the progressive study of New Testament Greek: the distinctive nature of *koiné* Greek (the language of the New Testament) was convincingly – if rather one-sidedly – demonstrated by Adolf Deissmann in his compelling book *Licht vom Osten.*51 This new wealth of textual material also influenced scholarly perspectives on daily life in antiquity, and on various forms of everyday but not officially sanctioned religiosity. In particular the so-called 'mystery religions' and the Mithras cult (especially popular among the military) now began to stand at the centre of attention.

Owing to the rapid pace of so many archaeological discoveries, a one-sided focus of attention often shifted quickly and fashionably from one location or source to the next. As a result, preliminary conclusions arising from successive discoveries did not always stand up to later, more considered scrutiny. The initial excitement that arose in Old Testament scholarship around Babylon (*Babel und Bibel!*) was quickly overshadowed by major finds at Ugarit; soon after that attention shifted to the archives of Ebla. During the first half of the 20th century, there was a 'Mandaean fever' among New Testament scholars: a feverish preoccupation with a trove of religious documents produced by a tiny, very ancient sect in Mesopotamia, in which John the Baptist figured prominently, and which led some to conjecture about deeper roots of Christianity. Since World War II, discoveries in the caves of Qumran, near the Dead Sea, including ruins of ancient monasteries and substantial remnants of ancient Essene texts, led to hasty conclusions: Christianity was declared to have been a successful variant of the Essene sect. In the meantime, attention shifted to the discoveries of gnostic (Coptic) texts at Nag Hammadi, and a revival of already long-standing interest concerning the place of *gnosis* in the historical origins of Christianity.

To some extent, the study of archaeological discoveries during the 20th century could arguably be seen as a continuation of the 17th century attention for parallel texts. The direction in which these fields of scholarship developed showed increasingly clearly that it is quite possible to study the world of the New Testament from widely different motives. While some scholars appeal to the outcomes of archaeological research to 'prove' that the Bible is right after all, others will draw on its findings to attempt to trace the historical-religious roots of Christianity.

Why does the recent study of the New Testament era lend itself more readily to such radically critical conceptions of ancient Christian history? Because of the rise of literary criticism (see further below) in the intervening period: historical data from the New Testament period is no longer linked to the acceptance of the New Testament as an integrated whole, but to separate or fragmentary pieces of its texts. Were one to take the New Testament as a unified whole, and compare it *as a whole* with Jewish apocalyptic literature of roughly the same period, the differences would be immediately obvious. If, however, one were to begin by reducing the Gospels to a collection of fragments of questionable authenticity, it becomes much easier to suggest that the 'ancient' or 'authentic' words of Jesus could have arisen within the atmosphere of Jewish apocalyptic tradition, with its highly-strung expectations concerning the future. Within this framework, someone like Albert Schweitzer placed all of Jesus' activity within Jewish apocalyptics, and therefore concluded that later developments after his death may largely be understood within the framework of reactions to a delayed end of the world (the so-called *Parusieverzögerung*): the initial eschatology cools and congeals into doctrinally focused epistles and historicised gospels.[52]

The 'history of religions' school, active since around 1880, found a prominent exponent in Wilhelm Bousset. While few may still regard his views on the whole as persuasive, his 'religious history' approach to the New Testament persists in a range of forms. For this reason, we conclude this section with a brief overview of the contents of his major work *Kyrios Christos* (1913).[53] As Bousset saw it, Christianity crystallized around the historical person Jesus of Nazareth, a prophet and miracle-worker in Israel. Outside the world of his time, the person of Jesus would never have led to the crystallization of a new world religion. Thanks to the influence of all kinds of religiosity at that time, Jesus (who henceforth was regarded as Christ) became the focus of a successful syncretism. The process by which this took place underwent a number of stages. It began with what could be described as a Palestinian root congregation. This gathering of adherents was saturated by an atmosphere of Jewish apocalyptic expectations; hence, it appropriated the title 'Son of Man', and applied it to the person of Jesus: true, Jesus has died, but at the end of time he will return as the long-awaited 'Son of Man'. When the Hellenistic-Gentile church adopts this belief, it 'translates' it into the more familiar categories of pagan cultic thinking, in which the Lord (Kyrios) of the cult is embodied within the cult itself. The expected Son of Man now becomes the venerated Kyrios. Later, Paul the theologian elevates this system of belief to a higher level, by constructing an elaborate supernatural doctrine of redemption upon and around it. And finally, the apostle John, influenced by Hellenist mysticism, recasts Christianity into an arcane, almost mystical religion. The original core of Jesus' teaching (the simple proclamation of a gracious and forgiving Father) has grown into an elaborate and many-faceted theological construction. It should be clear that in this conception Bousset incorporates beliefs from the (religious) world of the New Testament era, hand in hand with a critical reinterpretation of the writings of the prophets and evangelists.

The Study of the New Testament as Literature

It goes without saying that there has never been a time when exegetes did not, in their commentaries, examine the New Testament writings as a whole, and provide them with introductory remarks concerning their authors, time of writing, content overviews and the like. The first-century church fathers usually interwove such remarks with the exegesis itself; or else these remarks formed an introduction to their commentary on specific Bible books. In the New Testament manuscripts we often find, at the end of a gospel or an epistle, a few notes about the place from which they were sent, the author, etc. In later periods, such introductory material was often ordered into handbooks for the exegete, usually called *isagogues* (introductions). Hence, this kind of scholarly activity was often referred to as *isagogics:* the study of the authors, audience, content, etc. of the individual Bible books.

During the 17th and 18th centuries, isagogics expanded in scope and extent. It paid special attention to historic problems relating to dating and sequencing of the original texts. During the 19th and 20th centuries, however, this field of study was assigned an essentially different role and scope. What before was a purely *literary* introduction developed into a *literary-critical* introduction. The texts of the New Testament writings no longer formed the self-evident point of departure for Bible scholarship: now, the texts themselves were subjected to critical examination. Are these writings really what they purport to be? Might they perhaps have been an amalgam of material drawn from earlier sources? Are they really essentially different from other writings that could, together with them, be classified as 'early Christian literature'? The focus shifted from ascertaining the *place* of these texts to making judgements about their *worth*. Clearly this shift in emphasis is directly connected with the development of a critical view of the canon as such, and as a result of this shift, literary criticism now assumes a central, dominant position: the text of the Bible is no longer interpreted as it lies open before us; rather, it is filtered through the sieve of 'literary criticism'. Its wings are clipped, or it is dissected into isolated segments.

At the beginning of the 19th century, critical attention was initially directed towards the *historical authenticity* of the writings. Many scholars challenged the Mosaic origin of the Pentateuch. Chapters 40-66 of Isaiah were detached from their traditional source, the prophet Isaiah himself, and labelled as coming from a supposedly "deutero-Isaian" or even "trito-Isaian" source. In the New Testament, I Timothy and subsequently all of the pastoral letters began to be described as '*supposedly* Pauline', and not long after that the authorship of all the other letters of Paul and Peter was questioned. It will be clear that letting go of the authorial authenticity of the texts must necessarily have profound consequences. It may be compared to raising the anchor of a ship. Now that the document itself has been declared anonymous, it will soon be tossed about on the waves of hypotheses about origin, author, background, and so on.

A second point of contention soon arose: the *literary integrity* of the text. Important parts of the Bible (the Pentateuch, the Gospels) do not have a named author. The key, here, is not so much the historical *identity* of the author as the historical *accuracy* of the events described in these books. This becomes an issue when, in the process of questioning the sources of these writings, the literary integrity of the books themselves is left open to question.

I do not imagine that anyone has ever objected to the notion that the authors of the Pentateuch or the Gospels would, from time to time, have drawn on other, earlier sources. In fact, the books of Moses say so explicitly. But it is one thing to acknowledge that this is so; it is an entirely different matter to argue that the Pentateuch and the Gospels are in reality secondary sources, because they were totally dependent on primary sources, and will have compiled their story from these sources in human and sometimes quite questionable ways. We do not argue for the literary *originality* of every statement in the Bible; we do, however, affirm the literary *integrity* of the Bible books. It is this integrity that is undermined by various hypotheses concerning heterogeneous textual sources.

An example of such an hypothesis is that of the Pentateuch. There are scholars who suppose that it is in reality a synthesized compilation, variously of: a *prophetically* inclined Yahwist circle (J); a group inclined to *priestly* motivations (P); and a historicizing *deuteronomist* school(D).

Another example of this approach relates to the Gospels. Initially – so goes the hypothesis – the Gospels were supposed to have been compiled from a *Logia* source (Q), and from accounts about Jesus that go back to an earlier narrative source, thought by some to be the (proto)-gospel of Mark. The editors, Matthew and Luke, are thought to have used their own theological perspectives as a kind of 'glue' to bind the various heterogenous elements together. It will be clear that in this view it is no longer the literary document itself (in this case one of the Gospels) that dominates, but our own view of history in relation to the earliest period of Christianity. There will, of course, be a certain cross-pollination between critical study of the New Testament period and critical literary study of the text. However, that makes it no easier to ascertain whether the literary analysis provided is truly literary, and whether the historical analysis advanced is purely historical!

The third point that we wish to ask attention for relates to the *quality* of the books of the New Testament. We already observed that a departure from the authority of the canon will necessarily give rise to changes in such an evaluation. The New Testament itself then dissolves into little more than early Christian literature. Paul is then supposed to be the exponent of just one of many modalities in the early church: in reality, he ceases to be an apostle. His letters are no longer read as written 'by the will of Christ'; but as no more than letters 'from a human being and by a human being'. The Book of Acts, written to show how Jesus Christ carried on with his work, is then regarded as no more than a textual product of Luke, a theologian whose aim was to promote reconciliation between the 'Pauline line' and the 'Petrine line', and who in addition historicises a timeless eschatology by inserting an interim phase of 'the church'. The Gospels, products of tradition and redaction, become the pools that provide a shattered reflection of the multicoloured face of the early church.

It is often suggested that this evaluation of the quality of the text is no more than the inevitable outcome and necessary conclusions arrived *at the end* of a process of introductory scholarship. That, however, is simply not the case. In truth, this evaluation forms the *starting point* for this kind of activity. It is the wavelength chosen at the beginning that determines what is heard at the end. Much would be gained if this was openly acknowledged in the pursuit of these scholarly debates. In spite of statements to the contrary, modern handbooks in this field do not start out by accepting the Gospels and New Testament epistles as authentic and reliable, and regretfully concluding only after impartial research that this position is untenable. Instead, the reverse is true: an assessment of the quality of the text based on purely human standards is *a priori* imposed on it, and the possibility of divine inspiration is deliberately kept out of the picture. There will be no tears of grief when the conclusion is drawn that the Bible book being examined is regrettably not what it purports to be.

There is little point, then, for a structuralist exegesis to take its starting point in the integrity of the whole text as it presents itself to us. If at the same time, modern perspectives on introducing the text are upheld, and the conclusions arrived at from these perspectives prevail, such an integral approach to interpretation will have no choice but to treat the text as a literary abstraction, divorced from its history, inspiration, author and intended audience.

Since the literary-critical approach ignores the presentation and claims of the New Testament writings, there is little hope that the outcomes and conclusions of these different approaches will converge. Instead, evidence shows that in the introduction to each Bible book, a multitude of substitute hypotheses is developed and presented. There are no common conclusions, and even if there should be some agreement on points of detail, there never will be overall agreement in the long run.[54] This unavoidably raises the question: in reality, how scholarly is this approach?

The field of "Biblical theology".

A relatively new phenomenon in Biblical studies is the emergence of 'handbooks of Biblical theology', often further distinguished as 'theology of the Old Testament' and 'theology of the New Testament'. These works are usually sizeable tomes: scholars of theology will often regard such a work as the culmination of their career. Consequently, there are several incomplete theologies (such as those of Leonhardt Goppelt and Joachim Jeremias) to be found: the products of authors who did not live long enough to see the completion of their life's work. There are even elaborate studies of the whole field of 'Biblical Theology' itself.

To understand this boom in biblical theologies, we need to go back to the end of the 18th century. In 1787 Johann Philipp Gabler delivered an oration on the distinction between 'Biblical' and 'dogmatic' theology. In this address he advocated a theology that distanced itself from dogmatic or confessional points of departure, to the end that the theological conceptions found in Bible texts might be studied within a purely historical framework. In 'dogmatic theology' the Bible serves as the basis for dogmatics itself, while in 'Biblical theology', the *historic* development of theology in the Bible is given centre stage. Gabler would not have arrived at such an oration if he had not been convinced that there was a yawning chasm between the dogma of the Church and what the authors of the Bible themselves believed. Consequently, the 'canon-critical' perspective on the Bible demands a distinct theology of its own: the Bible is no longer regarded as the whole and single revelation of God, but as a varied collection of human documents, recording the faith experiences of people from the past.

Initially, New Testament theology limited itself to making an inventory of the theological thoughts expressed in each Bible book or by each of the apostles who wrote them. However, as literary criticism developed in the course of the 19th century (see above), the intent and design of 'New Testament theology' also changed. After all, there is little sense in ordering this kind of theology book by book, when the books themselves are turned upside down, divided into a variety of source documents, and these sources ranked by authenticity. In such a situation, theology sets itself two goals: first, to investigate, following on (!) from this critical scholarship, which theological developments accompanied the growth of the New Testament, and second, to determine what might be the most essential and authoritative cores of these early texts for later times.

A striking example of the second of these two goals is the well-known work of Adolf Von Harnack: *Das Wesen des Christentums* (1900; in English: *What is Christianity?*, 1901). Von Harnack presents as the essence and core of Christianity, Jesus' proclamation of the kingdom of God's paternal love, and the value of the human soul. In a certain sense, he identifies the tenets of 19th-century liberal theology precisely with what he conceives as the heart of the New Testament, and then proceeds to show how this Gospel is developed and encapsulated in history.

An example of the first of these goals is Rudolf Bultmann's sizeable *Theologie des Neues Testament* (1948; in English: *Theology of the New Testament*, 1961).[55] This work displays some notable similarities with Bousset's *Kyrios Christos* (see above). It traces Jesus' preaching, the kerygma of the earliest church, the kerygma of the Hellenist church before and next to Paul, Paul's own theology and that of John, as well as developments leading to the early Christian church. While Bousset seeks the core of this theology in its historical dimension (Jesus' simple preaching), Bultmann explores the theological dimensions of each phase of the development of early Christianity. As he understands it, each phase addresses in its own distinct manner a certain 'sense of being' (German: *Seinsverständnis*) that vibrates, as it were, in a variety of theological concepts. Throughout these various phases, the essential focus of early Christianity remains fixed on humanity's sense of self in this world. With the assistance of early Heideggerian concepts, Bultmann describes the theological dimensions of the various developmental phases in the New Testament.

Partly in opposition to the thoughts of Bultmann, the well-known New Testament scholar Oscar Cullman advocated that the concept of the 'history of salvation' be upheld in New Testament theology.[56] He did not want New Testament theology to lose itself in an a-historic *Selbstverständnis* (sense of self). As a constant theme among the various concepts in the New Testament he discerns the eschatological tension within which the reader knows himself to stand, living as he does between the 'already' and the 'not yet' of salvation. The dialectic between this 'already having come' of salvation and the 'not yet' attainment of perfection forms the area of tension within which all of the New Testament writers operate.

The manner in which such New Testament theology is practised usually reveals quite clearly that it is the resultant of preconceptions concerning the canon, the world of the New Testament, and the questions introductory to the examination of the text itself. Within the framework of New Testament criticism, a sum total of the worth of the text is calculated, be it positive or negative.

It seems strange that this kind of critical activity has retained the label of 'theology'. An historical description of *ideas about God* cannot exactly be regarded as theology! The term *theology* presupposes that GOD may be known, and that he is to be known through the revelation he himself gives concerning his existence and his attributes. Anyone who still proceeds from such an assumption would engage in an entirely different kind of study. After all, the first consequence of such an assumption would be that the Old and New Testaments are once again regarded as an organic unity, and it would not take long to discover that a 'Biblical theology' of this kind finds its way home to dogmatics, just as a prodigal son finds his way home to his father.

Over the course of time the subject 'New Testament theology' has become well-established, to the point where even those scholars who reject its points of departure will still strive for a kind of alternative, Scripturally bound 'New Testament theology'. Exponents of this approach include H.N. Ridderbos, G.E Ladd, D. Guthrie and L. Morris.[57] A large proportion of their work consists of a representation and evaluation of the theories of others. The extent to which it is even possible to adhere to this form ("a theology of the New Testament") while proceeding from different assumptions, and the degree to which this form, whether consciously or unconsciously, still acts as an obstruction or a distraction, is open to debate.

Summary and Conclusion

From the brief summary overviews of these three chief areas of study of modern Bible scholarship, as outlined in the foregoing, it is evident that the field of 'literary criticism' has a guiding role with respect to the other two. It is only when historical information concerning the world of the New Testament is combined with the results of this literary criticism that scholars can arrive at the conclusion that the Bible is largely the product of its own time, and not the fruit of divine revelation. On the other hand, it is also true that Biblical scholarship is often regarded as entirely dependent on the information presented to it by this literary criticism. And this scholarship is itself defined and determined by whether or not it submits to the authority of the canon. It would be fair to say that the whole practice of modern theology is directed by the presuppositions adopted in one's literary criticism.

In his *Encyclopedia of Sacred Theology*, Abraham Kuyper, reflecting on the methodology of Biblical theology, points to the decisive influence of the attitude one takes to the Bible's claim as Holy Scripture.[58] That was why Kuyper wouldn't have a bar of the term 'Introduction': such a term would imply neutrality and open-mindedness. Rather, he advocated the term 'Canonics' for this area of study, for such a term would convey that Bible scholarship deals with the *Canon*, with *Divine* Scriptures. In the sub-field of 'general canonics', that is the first part of canonics as whole, the scholar gives account of his attitude to the Canon: an attitude of acceptance or of rejection. Kuyper's own point of departure was that we do not need to prove the authority of the Canon; we must simply acknowledge the authority of Scripture, and give account of the way this authority functions for us. Modern Bible scholarship, which Kuyper rejects, camouflages this choice against the Canon by refusing to explicitly acknowledge it as a general and overarching principle, and by using an ostensibly neutral term 'literary criticism'. Indeed, it is quite striking that many handbooks of literary criticism devote only a limited number of pages to the Canon, and then only briefly as some sort of postscript: after all, it is not regarded as the starting point of theology; instead, it is no more than an addendum to the field.

In response to those who dismiss the authority of the Canon by appealing to a late completion of the Old Testament, or to only a gradual adoption of the New Testament Canon, we refer to Chapter 1 of this book. Based on what is discussed there, we may conclude that there are no compelling historical reasons to reject the authority of the Canon. Instead, everyone is inescapably confronted with the principal question regarding one's faith in the revelation of God (see ch. 1). The only possible conclusion is that an *a priori* choice against the authority of the Canon forms the point of departure of modern Bible scholarship, and that this starting point has wrongly been forced on the reader as a compelling conclusion. We cannot ground our belief in God's revelation on the outcomes of Bible scholarship, but there is no reason for us to surrender this belief because of the conclusions of 'literary criticism'.

No need for rigid defensiveness

In the foregoing, we have shown from a number of different perspectives that we cannot sidestep the authority of the Canon: we are not dealing with the product of synagogues and ecclesiastical councils, but with the preservation in written form of the revelation that God has given through his prophets and apostles. It is on this basis that the Church, through the ages, has received and passed on the Scriptures. Truly, concerning the Canon we accept what the apostle Paul wrote in Christ's name: *"All Scripture is breathed out by God and profitable for teaching, for reproof, for correction, and for training in righteousness, that the man of God may be competent, equipped for every good work"* (II Timothy 3:16,17). No matter how many persons may have been involved in that, in the end it is God himself who made the Bible for us. That obliges us to regard the Scriptures with reverence and awe. And that is something quite different from fearful or rigid defensiveness.

Fallible?

To many, the one great obstacle between the Canon and our believing acceptance of it is that the Bible seems to contain errors and shortcomings. Do not these blemishes betray that in the Bible we are confronted with (well-intentioned but fallible) human activity? Isn't the best we can say that God, at many times and in many ways, wants to use human material, because it forms a human record of our faith-experience?

Many works have been published which do not approach the books of Scripture from the starting point of an acceptance of their canonical authority, but from an analysis of their perceived errors and failings. It is these failings that would then determine the character of the Gospels, or of the Bible as a whole.[59] This activity could lead to a broad variety of conclusions. The enemies of Christendom, beginning with 4th century Neoplatonists, and continuing all the way to 21st century atheists, eagerly seize on these supposed failings in the Scriptures to rid themselves of the Bible altogether, dismissing it as a deceptive work, possibly an instrument of the capitalist phase of human history.

On the other hand, others may not necessarily arrive at such radical conclusions: instead, they attempt to save both the Bible and Christianity by retreating into a kind of *limited authority* of the Bible. This approach has many forms. The credibility of the Bible could be limited to a conjectured 'core canon' within the formal Canon of the church. Others could retreat into the 'intent' (the scope) of Scripture, while setting aside its whole historical structure. Still others might limit the authority of Scripture to what corresponds to one's own 21st-century faith experience.

There are also those who arrive at a new interpretation of the concept of 'organic inspiration'. In the past, this term was used to express that the authors of the Bible were not dehumanised by being reduced to some kind of dictation machine. The authors' own questions and emotional responses, sometimes even their protests, could be heard and felt. The term 'organic inspiration', which up till recently had always had a positive flavour, has now been given a quite different connotation. It suggests that the authors' organic engagement also implies that God did not progress beyond their errors and limitations. In fact, the word 'inspiration' itself evaporates. It would be much better to speak of the organic 'acceptance' of fallible authors. But no matter which terminology one might choose, or which approach one might take, in all these cases they lack the confidence to step into the Bible as the God-given canon of the Holy Scriptures. And such fears are only fed by the detection of perceived contradictions or errors encountered in the Bible.

Inerrant?

More or less as a reaction to this manner of dealing with the Bible, others defend the absolute faultlessness of Scripture. During the second half of the 20th century, especially in the USA, the word *'inerrancy'* has for many even become a kind of *shibboleth* for Biblical orthodoxy.[60] In their view, the only legitimate avenue of entry into Scripture is by way of adherence to a faultless inerrancy of the Bible.

Now it is undeniable that here and there we run into problems as we read the Bible. Sometimes it seems that we come across an error, an inconsistency or a contradiction. For example, when Matthew 27:9 quotes a text from Zechariah, and attributes it to Jeremiah, we are inclined at first glance to assume that Matthew was mistaken. Calvin raises the possibility that this is a transcription error. However, even then we must admit that the Bible, as it has been passed on to us, contains an error in this verse. Owing to this and other cases, some prefer to assert the inerrancy of the *original* manuscripts. Such a formulation, however, implies that the Bible, as we have it today, is not straightforwardly free of errors.

A large proportion of the problems that we encounter, however, are dismissed by the proponents of 'inerrancy' (faultless accuracy) as only apparent problems. Whole books have been published in which, going all the way from Genesis to Revelation, these problems are discussed and resolved.[61] The great value of these studies does not set aside their one great downside: the suggestion is created that our belief in the Canon rests upon an assertion of inerrancy, as if our faith in the Canon would necessarily disappear if even *one* error were to be found in it!

Trustworthy!

Still, are the problems that readers of the Bible might encounter on their way through the Scriptures of such weight that they would be decisively detrimental to our acceptance of the Canon? Must we feel *compelled* to reject, or strongly limit, the authority of the Canon because of contradictions we might find in the Bible? Or does our acceptance of the Canon require an *a priori* assumption on our part that the Bible is absolutely and faultlessly accurate? Any observer among us could easily gain this impression. There can be no doubt that a certain degree of rigidity has developed here. Many believers are being led to believe that, owing to the imperfections found in the Bible, we have no choice but to approach the Canon with a certain degree of reservation.

However, even without a detailed examination of all kinds of problems, we can say that the significance of such problems is often greatly exaggerated.

There really is no need to entrench oneself in a kind of 'doctrine of inerrancy' in order to calmly assume the credibility of the Canon. Our belief in the holy Scriptures does not require us to blush with embarrassment when we run into questions that cannot be readily resolved.

No cause for panic

Even in ordinary interactions among people, it does not follow that mistakes in detail necessarily compromise the credibility of one's story as a whole. It always depends on the nature of the errors, how significant they are, and how frequently they occur. If we were to catch the other repeatedly in inaccuracies or imagined details, then for us his credibility would diminish. At the same time, it is entirely possible that someone might give us a perfectly trustworthy account of certain events, while at the same time making a momentary misstatement or an obvious error. In such a case, there is no reason to claim that, because of this error of detail, the account as a whole must only be regarded in terms of its general intent, or that it probably didn't really happen like that. As we listen to each other, we maintain a sense of *proportion*.

The same thing is true of written records. We may come across historical accounts that are so riddled with errors, that we had better attach no value to their credibility at all. Narratives can be so tendentious that doubts must arise about their trustworthiness. On the other hand, it may also happen that we track down a number of errors of detail in Winston Churchill's *History of the Second World War*, while at the same time honouring this work as an extremely reliable account of the course of events. A spelling error ought not to lead the reader to conclude that the author is ignorant of the language he writes in, or is an advocate of 'free spelling'. In the same way, an historian might sometimes make an error that in no way affects his competence or trustworthiness as an historian.

As an example in real life: in 1860 a dissertation was published by a theological candidate, who died on 27 November 1859. One of his professors wrote a preface to this work, which contained all kinds of details about the author's life and deathbed, and dated it 6 January 1859.[62] An obvious error, one that is not uncommon: at the beginning of a new year, it is easy, by force of habit, to mistakenly write the previous year. Obviously, it would be an overreaction if a later reader (assuming the author's inerrancy) came to regard the preface as a prophecy, or (assuming the author's fallibility), dismissed the preface as an idealised account that ignored the facts of the deceased's life. No-one would be tempted to succumb to such an overreaction.

However, that is precisely what commonly happens with the Bible. There is a high degree of congruency between the accounts in the books of Kings and Chronicles. It is clear that these books, each from their very distinct perspective, describe the same events, and draw on the same historical sources. Still, it cannot be denied that there are problems.[63] The dating of the reigns of the respective kings can vary substantially. The names that are used are sometimes not congruent. However, an examination of these and similar problems, taking into account the coherence of these accounts as a whole, and their obvious concordance, provides no reason for panic. It really is not possible, based on these textual problems, to arrive at the conclusion that the authors might not have intended to provide an historical record. Even if we might not, for the time being, have a solution to these problems at hand, there is still no reason to attach sweeping consequences for the books as a whole to these differences in details.

The average layperson, when reading the Bible, often has a better sense of proportion in these questions than the specialist. The latter easily becomes fixated on such superficial blemishes, while everyone else looks at the person in question and simply sees a perfectly healthy and normal face. It is quite significant that many faithful readers of the Bible, when confronted with such issues, hold fast to their confidence in the trustworthiness of Scripture, even when they might not have an answer to any specific problem. While some might disparage that as a 'naïve' attitude, others would quite rightly see it as displaying a healthy sense of proportion. A dating error in a preface need not immediately unsettle the reader. Incidental problems in clear, transparent and largely consistent gospel accounts are no reason to attach less, or a different kind of, credence to what the evangelists present to us as history.

No superficial judgement

Whoever encounters a problem when reading a text ought to take care not to accuse the author too quickly of making an error. A snap conclusion or superficial judgement can so easily become injustice. Most of the 'contradictions' that people think they can find in the Bible evaporate only too quickly on calm and serious examination.

The fact that the name Goliath occurs in two separate contexts is sometimes quickly used to arrive at a generalized negative evaluation of the historic credibility of the two books of Samuel. Not only is that an overreaction, but in relation to this specific problem it is also a superficial judgement. In a Dutch ecclesiastical document (*Rapport 'God met ons'*, 1981) we read the following:

> "*Critical-historical study of the Bible has taught us to pay attention to the form of its stories. It has become apparent that not all literary genres we find in the Bible have similar degrees of historical accuracy. In a folk tale it really is not crucial who was actually the warrior who slew Goliath: David (I Samuel 17) or Elhanan (II Samuel 21:19). What matters in this account is the honour of God, who has miraculously delivered his people (cf. I Samuel 17:47). Which person played a role in this event is evidently less important than the triumph of God and his people.*"[64]

This passage assumes that both I Samuel 17 and II Samuel 21 talk about the same person Goliath. And this assumption leads to resounding conclusions. Still, to the author of both books of Samuel, it is extremely important who actually slew Goliath. At the beginning of his account of Goliath's death he makes a point of elaborately introducing David to the reader (I Sam 17:12-15; ch 17:30), and in a following place he comes back to it again: it was *David* who struck Goliath dead. (ch 21:9; 22:10). The story of David and Goliath does not come to us as the tale of some folk hero, but as unexpected – and all the more real – history, occurring in the context of a prophetic historical account that runs from Samuel to David. And now we run across the name of Goliath again, this time in II Samuel 21:20. Here we read that "*Elhanan, the son of Jaare-oregim the Bethlehemite, struck down Goliath the Gittite, the shaft of whose spear was like a weaver's beam*". This is not just a variant of the story about David recorded in I Samuel 17. This man is one of David's heroes, from a time long after Saul's death, and where king David is surrounded by courageous warriors (see I Chronicles 20). If it was true that the same Goliath is meant here, then we are faced with a larger problem than simply a degree of nonchalance about the identity of the chief character. The obvious conclusion must be that II Chronicles portrays an entirely different episode, and that the two accounts are mutually exclusive. It simply cannot be possible that the same Goliath was killed twice, with an intervening period of at least ten years. Not only that, but the totally different context of II Samuel 21 makes it clear that the name Goliath was fairly common. Might the name have been an honorific in the city of Gath for the city's champion? Could it have been a family name? In I Chronicles 20:5 we read that Elhanan slew the *brother* of Goliath, whose name was Lachmi. This raises further questions: could the name Goliath actually have been a title, which was passed from one brother to the next? As recently as the 20th century such a transfer of a name among contemporaries has still been known to occur.[65]

There is therefore no justification for a quick conclusion (one that conflicts with the thrust of both I Samuel 17 and II Samuel 21) that the same name Goliath automatically denotes the same person. This erroneous and far too hasty conclusion also blinds us for the numerous and significant differences between the narrative of David in I Samuel 17 and the reference to Elhanan in II Samuel 21 (a different location: the former at Soco, the latter in the region of Gob; the dates are different; the manner in which the death occurs is not the same: the former, a sling and a pebble, the latter, man-to-man combat; the significance of the events: the former, deliverance for Israel at a crucial moment, the latter, a consolidation of David's rule).

Now the advantage of a snap judgement is that just a few details allow for a quick and plausible conclusion. Anyone, however, who takes the trouble to do justice to all of the salient facts needs to tell a longer story, and thus risks tiring his audience.[66] Whenever we do not regard doing proper justice to Scripture as being worth the effort, we expose ourselves at the outset as partisan judges, with whom the Bible is not safe.

Keep a level head

Some readers, on discovering that questions may arise when reading the Bible, and that answers to these questions may not come readily to hand, might fall into a deep sense of confusion. Even so, this is a perfectly normal situation. Every written text assumes a great deal of prior knowledge on the part of the reader. Usually, listeners or readers can easily make sense of what they hear or read because they are contemporaries of the author. However, to the degree that there is a time shift between author and reader, there will be greater difficulty in comprehending the text. Allusions are no longer quite so transparent. Familiarity with earlier customs and practices recedes. Systems of measurement and numbering are no longer in common use. Archives and records get lost. And this leads to situations where texts that were quite problem-free for contemporaries give rise among later readers to questions which the original author could not have anticipated. The author would have taken for granted that his readers understood quite well how he counted the years of a king's reign. He would have taken for granted that using different names for the same person or the same place would not have presented readers with any problems, because 'everybody knew' the different names that some people or places went by. But would anyone still know 3000 years from now that 'the UK' and 'Britain' were different names for the same nation? Or that there were numerous Dutch kings who went by the name of 'William'? How many people would still be aware that a 'nautical mile' is considerably further than a mile on land? In the distant future, how many people would still know enough about European history to be aware that there is no discrepancy between Hitler and Stalin's war during the 1940's, and their non-aggression pact of 1939?

The Bible is full of things like these: after all, most of the Bible was written more than 2500 years ago. It is no wonder at all that we sometimes find it hard to make sense of all kinds of details. And it is quite likely that we, who have so much less first-hand knowledge than the first audience, sometimes run across what seem to us to be contradictions in the text.

No-one can tell us today where Matthew and Luke found the source material for their genealogies of Joseph, the descendant of David. To us, the widely varying lists of names appear to be quite incompatible (Matthew 1, Luke 3). Still, we would pay insufficient heed to the distance between ourselves and the gospels if we were to jump to the conclusion that the evangelists were indifferent to the historical accuracy of their genealogies. In fact, both of the evangelists are at pains to present the facts of history in order to demonstrate that Joseph, in whose household Jesus was born, was a true descendant of David. If they had simply written down an imaginary list of names, would that not have had a counterproductive effect upon their readers, who would certainly have understood how proofs of genealogical descent worked (see Ezra 2:59-63)? Moreover, we should consider that quite different genealogical records covering lengthy periods often intersect at numerous points. Since brothers generally do not marry their own sisters, the lines of descent might diverge widely at first, while after the passage of time two people who might be very distantly related could marry. In this way, two lines of descent could easily converge again. Hence, there is really no reason to *a priori* regard with suspicion one or the other of the genealogies in the gospels: yes, the names that are recorded differ widely, but that is exactly what happens with two widely diverging lines of descent. Where the names coincide, they coincide in sequence. Each of the evangelists would have wanted to accentuate certain highlights: you can tell a whole story by following a particular line of descent! But the fact of our unfamiliarity with numerous names in these lists, and of our ignorance of the sources the evangelists drew on (especially when we consider the time interval that has elapsed since then), gives us no reason at all to assume that the evangelists played fast and loose with historical facts.[67]

It is precisely because the Bible is a book that does not deal with abstract and timeless assertions, but is rooted in the history of God's dealings with his people during the passage of days and years, that the credibility of Scripture cannot be contingent on whether or not it appears to be inerrant to us. That's not because the Bible is subject to human error, but because his written revelation, just like any other written text, might be easily misunderstood or misinterpreted over the passage of time, and at first glance may *appear* to us to be in error.

A test case: Christ's cleansing of the temple.

The credibility of the Canon has its basis in the reality of God's revelation in this world. It would be wrong to claim that this credibility depends on our ability to resolve some questions that arise for us as we read the Bible. We would like to address one such 'problem' here, but not with the intention of somehow 'proving' the Bible's credibility. In fact, the reverse is the case. The Biblical record of this event is often used as a test case to show that the Bible's account is *not* credible.

In his *Escaping from Fundamentalism* the liberal Old Testament scholar James Barr attempts to show that a historical reading of the Bible compels us to accept a less canonical characterization of Scripture. He begins by using a 'simple example'.[68] Precisely this same example is used in the report *"God met Ons"* in order to demonstrate that 'accurate historiography' was not the prime purpose of the evangelists; rather, argues the report, what impelled them was a *'certain interpretation of the life of Christ as the fulfilment of the Old Testament Scriptures'*.[69]

The significance of the test case is greater than it is sometimes portrayed. The *"God met Ons"* report tends to gloss over the matter by putting it this way: *"The question whether the cleansing of the temple took place at the beginning of Jesus' ministry* (John 2) *or near its end* (Matthew 21:12-13; Mark 11:15-18; Luke 19:45-48) *carried less weight with the evangelists than we would generally be inclined to think"*. And a little later we read that the positioning of this event in an *interpretation* of Jesus' life would *"of course not imply that this account is not based on an actual event that took place in the temple"*. But why is that 'of course' not? If we cannot accept the evangelists' report as historically reliable, then for what kind of self-evident or natural reason must we accept that Jesus was ever in the temple at all, or that he actually did cleanse it of traders and money-changers? Who then decides what did or did not 'of course' happen? Why should the authority of a centuries-later synod come to our assistance when the historical authority of the evangelists is set aside? At least Barr's formulation is more outspoken, when he spells out the consequences of accepting a view that John and the other evangelists presented an historically inaccurate account of the cleansing of the temple. He draws attention to the 'immense effect' that this matter has for our perspective on the Gospels, for it is now *"at one stroke clear that they, or at least some of them, did not simply narrate what is historically true."*[70] Barr quite rightly attaches profound consequences to this test case. Should it become evident that one or more evangelists knowingly violated historical truth, then one might still charitably characterize their story as an 'interpretation', but it shouldn't surprise us at all if readers of the Bible, on hearing this assertion, no longer give any credence to the evangelists' account. After all, this is not just a matter of a minor discrepancy. We would be compelled to believe that one or more of the apostles *knowingly* recounted events as they *did not* happen. It is worthwhile to examine this test case rather more closely.

In John 2:13-25, right at the beginning of his Gospel, we find the narrative of Jesus' actions in the temple in Jerusalem. It is during a visit to

Jerusalem, at the time of the Passover, that Jesus drives herds of sheep and cattle out of the temple court, and overthrows the tables of the money-changers. The sellers of pigeons are ordered to remove their merchandise: *"Take these things away! Do not turn my Father's house into a house of trade!"* This is also the time at which Jesus utters his well-known word: *"Destroy this temple, and in three days I will raise it up"*.

We find a similar account of a cleansing of the temple with the other three evangelists. But now, they place it at the very end of Jesus' ministry. During his final Passover visit to Jerusalem, just before his passion and death, Jesus drove the merchants out of the temple. *"Isn't it written, 'My house shall be a house of prayer?' But you have made it a den of robbers!"* (Matthew 21:12-17: Mark 11:15-19; Luke 19:45-48).

While the first three evangelists do not tell anything about a cleansing of the temple at the *beginning* of Jesus' public ministry, John says nothing about such a cleansing at the *end*. This could plausibly lead to the conclusion that there would have been just *one* such cleansing: not one of the evangelists says anything about *two* such events. However, if that were true, it must mean that one or the other event is dated quite incorrectly. There is an interval of not less than three full years between the *beginning* of Jesus' public ministry and its *end*.[71] Anyone who relocates this event from the beginning of Jesus' activity to its end, or *vice versa*, radically separates it from its historical context. It is usually John who is identified as the one who has carried out this historical shift, owing to his personal objectives in writing his Gospel.

If we accept that this is what John did, we would be forced to conclude that he had dismantled the true course of history. It might not matter so much if John had merely narrated this event *out of sequence*, and left the details intact. After all, an author has every right to shift the *sequencing* of events in a narrative structure. Authors do that all the time, in the interests of literary composition, and that is quite legitimate, as long as it is clear that the *narrative* sequence is not the same as the *chronological* sequence of events. But in this case, it's not so simple. After all, John not only *sequences* this event earlier in his narrative; he also quite explicitly *dates* it much earlier. In John 2 we read that the cleansing of the temple took place *just after* the miraculous turning of water into wine at the wedding at Cana, and *before* Jesus' conversation with Nicodemus (John 2:1,12,13,23; ch 4:45). John explicitly points out that the cleansing of the temple took place during this period in Jesus' ministry, and so excludes the possibility that we could regard this event as a thematically ordered account of what actually took place at a later date.

Now we know that John had personal and independent knowledge of the earliest phase of Jesus' ministry. It even seems possible that he kept a diary (John 1:29,35; ch 2:1). He relates events that other evangelists don't mention or wouldn't have known about (John 1:19-5:47). Doesn't this strongly suggest that we ought to take him seriously as an historian, also when he tells the story of the cleansing of the temple? John knew what he was writing about; after all, he had been following the activities of Jesus from the earliest beginning, already as a disciple of John the Baptist. Were it not for the fact that *all three* other evangelists place their accounts of the cleansing of the temple near the end of Jesus life on earth, there would have been no reason to doubt John's much earlier date.

At the same time, there is no reason to believe that the other evangelists might have *shifted* the account of the cleansing of the temple to the end of Jesus' ministry. It fits with his entry into Jerusalem, and is linked directly to the challenge of the Jewish leaders concerning his authority.

The idea that Jesus might have cleansed the temple *twice* is dismissed as contrived by numerous scholars. Now it must be acknowledged that an event like the temple cleansing is less likely to have been repeated than many of Jesus' healings, discourses or disputes. On the other hand, it is not uncommon that something which is unlikely did still really happen. Historically, a repeated cleansing of the temple is by no means impossible.

There is more to be said. The words that Jesus spoke about breaking down the temple, and rebuilding it within three days, fit quite well with John's account of the temple cleansing. They do not occur on the second occasion. Did Jesus really utter these words at the beginning, and not at the end of his period of activity? We may accept that this is the case, when we consider the statements of the false witnesses at Jesus' trial before the Jewish council. Near the end of the hearing, after numerous other witnesses have been heard, two witnesses come forward, and they report what Jesus had said about 'breaking down the temple'. Even so, the matter is not clear-cut: when their statements are tested for agreement concerning the time, place, etc. of Jesus' reply, it turns out that they are inconsistent (Mark 14:55-59). A scene such as this one is hardly imaginable if Jesus had said such a thing in the temple courtyard, in everyone's hearing, only a few days earlier. After all, everyone had witnessed this shocking statement themselves! The problem of those two false witnesses reveals that their memory goes back to something that had happened much earlier. They might not be certain about the exact details anymore, but they do remember the gist of what Jesus had said about breaking down the temple. It is precisely because Jesus' statement functions as a hazy memory of something that has been dug up from the distant past, that it must have occurred much longer ago than his entry into the city a few days earlier. And this confirms the accuracy of John's account. In the same way as Christ's act of cleansing the temple, his word about breaking down the temple may be dated from the beginning of his ministry: a beginning that people still remember, but only vaguely, at its end. The account by the first three evangelists of Jesus' trial indirectly confirms John's report of what had happened years earlier. In addition to the clearing of the temple at the end, there must have been an earlier, similar event, where Jesus spoke about the temple. If, as John reports, this had taken place near the beginning of Jesus' ministry, it is quite understandable that initially no-one had taken it very seriously: after all, at that time Jesus had not yet been a suspect, whose movements and activities were constantly monitored by the Sanhedrin.

When we subject both events to closer comparison, we notice even more differences. In John 2, there is no reference to the '*den of robbers*' that is so characteristic of the second clearing of the temple. Jesus' use of the term 'den of robbers' fits well with the end of his ministry: the Jewish Council is lying in wait to trap Jesus, to arrest him, and to put him to death. In these last days of heightened hostility, Jesus shows that he sees through the intentions of the Jewish leaders. In addition, he shows that by their actions, it is they who are defiling the temple. The temple is the house of prayer to God for all nations, but they have turned it into a base of operations for murderers, and because of this the last hour of the temple has come. Jesus portrays this impending judgement by driving out the traders with their sacrificial animals from the temple courtyard. He even shuts down the normal traffic on the great temple square (Mark 11:16): business grinds to a halt when they will not accept the Saviour, but instead attack him! The clearing of the temple at the beginning of Jesus' ministry does not yet have such a threatening and judgemental aspect. On that occasion, there is no evidence that normal traffic had been brought to a halt. Not only that, but at that time Jesus' actions were directed much more closely to the sacrificial animals. This is clear from a small detail: Jesus fashioned a whip of cords, and used it to drive the animals out of the courtyard (John 2:15). There is no mention of a whip on the second occasion: he doesn't accost people with a whip; that is used on animals! *"Making a whip of cords, He drove them all out of the temple, with the sheep and oxen"*. It wasn't his intention to destroy the merchandise: he did not release the pigeons; no, he ordered the sellers to remove them from the temple (John 2:16). Why? Because his Father's house should not be made into a house of trade. Here, Jesus doesn't call the temple 'a den of robbers', but 'a house of trade'. Jesus wanted to put an end to the buying and selling of sacrificial animals. Why was that? It is not till later that the disciples understand his intention: Jesus has come to present *himself* as the Lamb of God (John 1:29, 36). After all, it is written: *"Zeal for Your house will consume me"* (John 2:17). In the place of sacrificial animals, which at present are just merchandise, Jesus will present himself as a sacrifice for sin. That is how he will enter as Son into the house of his Father, as a Lamb in the temple. The fact the Jesus enacts this first sign in the temple, symbolic of the plan for his life, becomes evident from the Word that he speaks. Instead of this temple of stone, a temple that may and will be broken down, he will raise a new temple, after three days. In this statement, Jesus alludes to his death and resurrection. The temple of his body, broken for the sins of the world, is close at hand. When he has come, the trade in sacrificial animals will be abolished. His Father's house is no longer a house of trade, but a house of grace, brought about by his sacrificial death. Later, his disciples would come to understand. Already at this early point in his ministry he could shut down the trade in merchandise, and send the sacrificial animals home, for he himself would be consumed because of his zeal for his Father's house.

On closer examination, there is a great deal of difference between the first cleansing of the temple and the second. The latter is a sign of judgement upon the Jewish leaders who, for the sake of their temple, are plotting to destroy him.

Our conclusion is that it is worth the effort to take our starting point in the evangelists' credibility. Our eyes are then open to the splendid nuances within Jesus' activity, and we are safeguarded from oversimplifying the history presented in Scripture, and indeed from casting doubts upon its trustworthiness.

Conclusion

The problems we run into as we read the Bible are there to be confronted according to our ability, in a manner that is respectful of Holy Scripture, and without closing our eyes to the questions which may arise. There is a certain value, for the encouragement of the reader, in searching for answers to such questions, and in resolving exegetical problems. Before we engage in such study, however, we are faced with a choice: do we believe in the almighty power of God, and do we accept the authority of his revelation? Or do we refuse to take a stand upon it? That is the *a priori* question that this book chiefly addresses. For further discussion of certain concrete problems, I must refer to other works.

The subject discussed here is of fundamental importance for Christianity. Anyone who contests the historical trustworthiness of the Canon is in fact sawing off the limb upon which he sits. There is only a limited time in which to choose between confessional Christianity and a modern Scripture-critical Christianity. Sooner or later the choice we make is superseded by a choice for or against the Christian faith itself. Without confidence and trust in the Scriptures, as they have been passed on to us by the prophets and apostles, our faith in God and in his Son Jesus Christ will deviate from its proper course, and will miss its safe haven.

ENDNOTES

1 For a broad discussion of the term 'canon' in ecclesiastical usage during first centuries of the church see Heinz Ohme, *Kanon Ekklesiastikos: Die Bedeutung des altkirchlichen Kanonbegriffs* (Arbeiten zur Kirchengeschichte 67; Berlin 1998).

2 See Paul R. Noble, *The Canonical Approach: A critical Reconstruction of the Hermeneutics of Brevard S. Childs* (Leiden 1995); Robert W. Wall; Eugene E. Lemcio, *The New Testament as Canon: A Reader in Canonical Criticism*. JSNT SS 76 (Sheffield 1992); Robert W. Wall, „Canonical Criticism" (in: Stanly E. Porter (ed.), *Handbook to Exegesis of the New Testament*, pp. 291-312; New Testament Tools and Studies 25. [Leiden 1997]).

3 For a discussion of the content of these passages see „Marcus 13 en de profetieën van Daniël" in my *Marcus: het evangelie volgens Petrus* (Kampen: Kok, 1988), pp. 405-412.

4 In my study *Wie maakte de bijbel? Over afsluiting en gezag van het Oude en Nieuwe Testament* (Kampen: Kok, 1986) the Council of Jamnia is discussed on pp. 26-27 and the inclusion of Ecclesiastes and the Song of Songs in pp. 114-119 (Excursus A).

5 Flavius Josephus, *Contra Apionem* 1,28-29. Translated into English by William Whiston, 1926, www.fulltextarchive.com/page/Against-Apion/

6 *c. Apionem* 1,37.

7 *c. Apionem* 1,38

8 *c. Apionem* 1,39-40.

9 *c. Apionem* 1,41.

10 *c. Apionem* 1,42-43.

11 4 Ezra 14,18-48.

12 We find the same threefold division in Philo (*De vita contemplativa 25*) and in Luke 24:44

13 I Maccabees 12:9 also refers to "*the holy books of Scripture we have in our hands*" in a manner that assumes a well-defined whole.

14 O. Eissfeldt, *Einleitung in das Alte Testament usw.* (Tübingen, ³1964) p. 706.765-766.

15 David Trobisch, *Die Endredaktion des Neuen Testaments: Eine Untersuchung zur Entstehung der christlichen Bibel;* Novum Testamentum et Orbis Antiquus 31 (Freiburg 1996), p. 5-11. Trobisch investigated the appearance and literary cohesion of the NT texts in ancient manuscripts: in them he identifies certain editorial characteristics, suggesting a tendency towards uniformity which according

to him point to one early edition underlying the corpus that we call 'the New Testament'. However, his conclusions are not supported by his contemporaries.

16   H. Fr. von Campenhausen, *Die Entstehung der christlichen Bibel* (Tübingen 1968) pp. 143-144 (translation mine, AP).

17   Barnabas, *Epistle*. This and following translations of Barnabas by JB Lightfoot, 1891, retrieved from: http://www.earlychristianwritings.com/text/barnabas-lightfoot.html

18   Clement *Second Epistle*. This and following translations of Clement by JB Lightfoot, 1891, retrieved from: http://www.earlychristianwritings.com/2clement.html

19   Ignatius, *Second Epistle to the Ephesians*. Translation by A Roberts and J Donaldson in: *The Ante-Nicene Fathers, Vol. 1*. Buffalo, NY: Christian Literature Publishing Co., 1885.) Retrieved from: http://www.newadvent.org/fathers/0104.htm

20   Ignatius, *Epistle to the Philadelpians*, This and following translations of Ignatius by JB Lightfoot, 1891. Retrieved from http://www.earlychristianwritings.com/text/ignatius-philadelphians-lightfoot.html

21   Eusebius, *Historia Ecclesiastica* III 39, 15-17.

22   Eusebius, *Historia Ecclesiastica* III, 39. This and following translations of Eusebius by AC McGiffert. *From Nicene and Post-Nicene Fathers, Second Series*, Vol. 1. Edited by Philip Schaff and Henry Wace. (Buffalo, NY: Christian Literature Publishing Co., 1890.)

23   A. von Harnack, *Marcion: Das Evangelium vom fremden Gott. Eine Monographie zur Geschichte der Grundlegung der katholischen Kirche* (Leipzig 1921).

24   J. Knox, *Marcion and the New Testament* (Chicago 1942).

25   See for example Lee M. McDonald, *The Formation of the Christian Biblical Canon,* Revised and Expanded Edition (Peabody 1996), p. 160.

26   E.C. Blackman, *Marcion and His Influence* (London 1948).

27   Origen, *Comm. Rom.* 10,43 (MPG 14,1290). For a broader discussion of this passage see my *Het raadsel van Romeinen 16: De apostel Paulus en het ontstaan van de kerk te Rome* (Groningen 1970), pp. 37-46.

28   Tertullian: *Adversus Marcionem*. This and following translations of Tertullian by Peter Holmes. *From Ante-Nicene Fathers, Vol. 3*. Edited by Alexander Roberts, James Donaldson, and A. Cleveland Coxe. (Buffalo, NY: Christian Literature Publishing Co., 1885.)

29   In my *Wie maakte de bijbel? Over afsluiting en gezag van het Oude en Nieuwe Testament* (Kampen: Kok, 1986, no longer in print) I discussed the influence of both Origen and Eusebius on the New Testament canon. (pp.120-138)

30   A. Wikenhauser: J. Schmid, *Einleitung in das Neue Testament* (Freiburg 1973), p. 50 (translation mine, AP)

31   Athanasius, *Paschal letter*. Translation of this and following excerpts from Athanasius: R. Payne-Smith: *From Nicene and Post-Nicene Fathers, Second Series, Vol. 4*. Edited by Philip Schaff and Henry Wace. (Buffalo, NY: Christian Literature Publishing Co., 1892.)

32 W.G. Kümmel, *Einleitung in das Neue Testament* (Heidelberg ¹⁷1973), p. 442 (translation mine, AP).

33 E.J. Jonkers (ed.), *Acta et Symbola Conciliorum quae saeculo quarto habita sunt* (Textus Minores XIX; Leiden 1974), p. 136.

34 *De viris illustribus* 10 (MPL 23, 657).

35 Further elaboration at this point can be found in my *Ambten in de apostolische kerk: een exegetisch mozaïek* (Kampen 1984), pp. 37-59. 62-64

36 Josephus, (*Contra Apionem* 1: 29, 37-38).

37 Tertullian, *Apology*, 20, tr. TH Bindley.

38 Christoph Dohmen, ``Vom vielfachen Schriftsinn – Möglichkeiten und Grenzen neuerer Zugänge zu biblischen Texten" (in: Thomas Sternberg (ed.), *Neue Formen der Schriftauslegung?* 13-74, Quaestiones Disputatae 140 [Freiburg 1992]). Dohmen summarizes his argument as follows: 'From fourfold to manifold meaning of Scripture!" (p.67).

39 An exhaustive study of this subject is to be found in the four-volume work of Henri de Lubac: *Exégèse Médiévale:Les quatre sens de l'Écriture* (Paris 1959 [Première partie]. 1961-1964 [Seconde partie]).

40 Not just in the triad 'Faith, Hope and Love', but also in the trinitarian and redemptive-historical triad of Israel (faith in God), Church (the love of Christ) and Fatherland (hope in the heavenly homeland of the Spirit).

41 Secundum igitur primam significationem, quae est per voces, accipitur sensus literalis, vel historicus; secundum vero aliam significationem, quae est per ipsas res, accipitur sensus mysticus, seu spiritualis, qui est triplex in generali" (MPL 113, 28) *"The first of these two meanings lies in the words, and this gives us the literal or historical sense; the other meaning lies in the reality described by these words, and this gives us the mystical or spiritual sense, which is usually threefold."* (MPL 113, 28) (translation mine from the Dutch, AP)

42 Maximino Arias Reyero, *Thomas von Aquin als Exeget: Die Prinzipien seiner Schriftdeutung und seine Lehre von den Schriftsinnen* (Sammlung Horizonte, Neue Reihe 5; Einsiedeln 1971).

43 In his *Summa Theologica I, question 1, Article 10,* Thomas considers the objections that a multiple meaning of the text gives rise to confusion, and undermines argumentation based on the text; further, that it is illogical to assert that one text could have a plurality of meanings. He summarizes his general response to such objections as follows: *"The author of Sacred Scripture is God, who has it in His power to use not only words for signifying (which even a man can do), but also the very things themselves. And so even though words are used to signify in all the sciences, it is peculiar to the science of sacred doctrine that the thing signified by the words likewise signify something themselves. Thus, the first type of signification, by which words signify things, pertains to the first sense, which is the historical or literal sense. On the other hand the type of signification by which the things signified by words in turn signify other things, is called the spiritual sense, which is built upon the literal sense and presupposes it".* (A Freddoso: *New English Translation of Thomas Aquinas' Summa Theologiae,* Notre Dame, IN, USA, University of Notre Dame, www3.nd.edu/~afreddos/summa-translation/TOC-part1.htm, accessed 21 02 2018).

44   C.J. den Heyer, „Geschiedenis van de exegese vanaf de Reformatie tot heden" (in: *Bijbels Handboek*, deel 3: Het Nieuwe Testament, 561-598; Kampen 1987).

45   C.J. den Heyer, „Geschiedenis van de exegese vanaf de Reformatie tot heden" (in: *Bijbels Handboek*, deel 3: Het Nieuwe Testament, 561-598; Kampen 1987), p. 561 (translation mine, AP).

46   W.G. Kümmel, *Das Neue Testament im 20. Jahrhundert: Ein Forschungsbericht* (Stuttgart 1970), p.8 (translation mine, AP)..

47   Kummel: „eine wissenschaftliche Erforschung des Neuen Testaments im strengen Sinne des Wortes", p. 8

48   For more elaborate descriptions see: W.G. Kümmel, *Das Neue Testament. Geschichte der Erforschung seiner Probleme* (Freiburg ²1970). S. Neill; T. Wright, *The Interpretation of the New Testament 1861-1986* (Oxford 1988). H.J. Genthe, *Kleine Geschichte der neutestamentlichen Wissenschaft* (Göttingen 1977).

49   H.L. Strack, P. Billerbeck, *Kommentar zum Neuen Testament aus Talmud und Midrasch*. IV Bande (München 1922-1928). Two volumes of indices were later added.

50   Novum Testamentum Graece, nec non commentario pleniore ex scriptoribus veteribus hebraeis, graecis et latinis etc. 1751-2.

51   *Licht vom Osten: Das Neue Testament und die neuentdeckten Texte der hellenistisch-römischen Welt* (Tübingen ⁴1923).

52   *Von Reimarus zu Wrede: Eine Geschichte der Leben-Jesu-Forschung* (Tübingen ²1913).

53   *Kyrios Christos. Geschichte des Christusglaubens von den Anfängen des Christentums bis zu Irenaeus* (Göttingen 1913). For more information on Bousset, see: A.F. Verheule, *Wilhelm Bousset, Leben und Werk; Ein theologiegeschichtlicher Versuch* (Amsterdam 1973).

54   Those who wish to explore this field further would do well to consult a handbook that focuses primarily on creating an inventory of existing views, rather than the development of new hypotheses. Critical texts from a Protestant perspective include: W.G. Kümmel, *Einleitung in das Neue Testament* (Heidelberg ²⁰1980). A useful modern work from a Roman Catholic perspective is: A. Wikenhauser; J. Schmid, *Einleitung in das Neue Testament* (Freiburg ⁶1973). More conservative works, representative for an 'evangelical approach', include: D. Guthrie, *New Testament Introduction* (London ³1970), and D.A. Carson; Douglas J. Moo; Leon Morris, *An Introduction to the New Testament* (Grand Rapids 1992). For a contemporary survey, see: Eldon Jay Epp, George W. MacRae (eds.), *The New Testament and Its Modern Interpreters* (Philadelphia/Atlanta 1989).

55   Bultmann, R: *Theology of the New Testament*. Waco, USA, 2007.

56   O. Cullmann, *Heil als Geschichte. Heilsgeschichtliche Existenz im Neuen Testament* (Tübingen 1965).

57   H.N. Ridderbos, *De komst van het koninkrijk: Jezus' prediking volgens de synoptische evangeliën* (Kampen 1950). *Paulus: Ontwerp van zijn theologie* (Kampen 1966). G.E. Ladd, *A Theology of the New Testament* (Grand Rapids 1974). D. Guthrie, *New Testament Theology* (Leicester 1981). Leon Morris, *New Testament Theology* (Grand Rapids 1986).

58 A. Kuyper, *Encyclopaedia of sacred theology*, Vol. III (New York, Scribners, 1898), p. 22ff.

59 See for example: J. Barr, *Escaping from Fundamentalism* (London 1984); Tj. Baarda, *De betrouwbaarheid van de evangeliën* (Kampen 1967).

60 See for example: H. Lindsell, *The Battle for the Bible* (Grand Rapids 1976). Compare also the discussion that erupted among Evangelicals with the publication of Robert H Gundry's *Matthew, a Commentary on His Literary and Theological Art* (Grand Rapids 1982), notably in *Journal of the Evangelical Theological Society* 26 (1983) 3-136 and *The Evangelical Quarterly* 55 (1983) 129-144.177-180. See also various articles in *Journal of the Evangelical Theological Society* 25 (1982) 385-506, and an anthology in: Douglas Moo (ed.) *Biblical Authority and Conservative Perspectives: Viewpoints from Trinity Journal*; Biblical Forum Series 1 (Grand Rapids 1997).

61 G.L Archer: *Encyclopedia of Bible Difficulties* (Grand Rapids, 1982).

62 *De kennis der geloovigen. Laatste leerrede van Heine Jacobs Ritzema, in leven candidaat aan de Theol. School te Kampen. Met een woord over den ontslapene door A. Brummelkamp, leeraar aan de Theol. School te Kampen* (Kampen 1860).

63 See, for example, J. Barr, *Fundamentalism* (London 1977) p. 281.

64 *Rapport God met ons, over de aard van het Schriftgezag. Special Kerkinformatie* no. 113 (Leusden). *See* p. 65. Barr also discusses this example in his, *Fundamentalism* (London 1977) pp. 281-282.

65 A fairly recent example is that of the late president of North Korea, Kim Il-sung (1912-1984). His actual name was Kim Song-ju. Prior to him, a number of Korean resistance leaders went by the name Kim Il-sung, and by adopting this name, Kim Song-ju aimed to appropriate the 'immortality' of his predecessors.

66 In the *Rapport:'God met ons'* (p. 65) we read: "*Anyone who wishes (! JvB) to assign a high degree of historical reliability to ancient Israelite texts, since even the lapses of the greatly admired kings David and Solomon are not omitted, should remember that in* Chronicles *these facts are suppressed*" (translation mine, AP). This highly suggestive statement refers to the fact that David's sin with Bathsheba is not recorded in *Chronicles*. However, why should that be a significant omission? *I and II Samuel* together contain 38 chapters dealing with the life of David, including two references to culpable actions (David's sin with Bathsheba and the numbering of the people), while *I Chronicles* consists of 18 chapters about David, with one reference to a sinful action (the counting of David's army). The frequency of such lapses is quite comparable in *Samuel* and *Chronicles*. Besides, every reader of the Bible ought to be aware that the author of *Chronicles* highlights the holiness of temple worship, and by no means glosses over sins in the Davidic line of kings.

67 The report "*God met ons*" makes a vague reference to this: "*The trustworthiness of Old Testament depends, not so much on historical research, as on the assurance of faith*" (p.75, Translation mine, AP)

68 J. Barr, *Escaping from Fundamentalism* (London 1984) p. 68.

69 Report '*God met ons*' p. 77-78.

70 J. Barr, *Escaping from Fundamentalism* (London 1984) p. 68.

71 J. van Bruggen, „*Na veertien jaren". De datering van het in Galaten 2 genoemde overleg te Jeruzalem* (Kampen 1973) pp. 65-113. H.W. Hoehner, *Chronological Aspects of the Life of Christ* (Grand Rapids ²1978) pp. 45-63.

www.ingramcontent.com/pod-product-compliance
Lightning Source LLC
Chambersburg PA
CBHW070736020526
44118CB00035B/1390